NOTHING WASTED

GOD USES THE STUFF YOU WOULDN'T

STUDY GUIDE | SIX SESSIONS

KASEY VAN NORMAN

ZONDERVAN®

ZONDERVAN

Nothing Wasted Study Guide
© 2019 by Kasey Van Norman

978-0-310-10420-9 (softcover)
978-0-310-10421-6 (ebook)

Requests for information should be addressed to
Zondervan, *3900 Sparks Dr. SE, Grand Rapids, MI 49546*

Published in association with literary agent Jenni Burke of D.C. Jacobson & Associates LLC, an Author Management Company www.dcjacobson.com.

Cover illustration: Dana Tanamachi
Interior designer: crosslincreative.net

First Printing September 2019 / Printed in the United States of America

CONTENTS

A NOTE FROM ME TO YOU

Well hello there, love. Welcome. And may I be the first to say thank you. Truly and from the bottom of my heart.

Perhaps you're reluctantly showing up for the first time and already rehearsing the reasons why you don't plan to show up again. Maybe you're surrounded by trusted companions, doing your best to knee-balance a plate of tonight's potluck dinner mix (around which you unashamedly stacked store-bought mini-muffins in lieu of the home-prepared veggie tray). Perhaps, like me at this very minute, you're propped up against a pillow in bed, alone with your thoughts for the first time today, hoping this study might create some semblance of order amidst the chaos.

However and whenever our hearts meet in this crazy world, I am more grateful for you than you will ever know. Whether you're among friends, alone in a crowded room, or alone at your kitchen table, I trust the Lord has brought us together at this exact moment in time to believe him more fully than we ever have before!

In fact, I've been thinking about you for a long time. I've been sure that if this project ever made it to print, it would only be because God himself had prepared a rare and wonderful kind of human to work through it. A human whose life story completely validates the entire premise of this work, but also someone with just enough ache and desperation in their heart that they are willing to risk everything on the possibility God is exactly who he says he is. If you are reading these words right this very minute, I feel compelled to let you in on a secret, *"Pssst. It's you."*

Perhaps, as I once did, you feel your backstory is either too scandalous or too boring to be used by God in a powerful way. If this is you, I get it. I really do.

After years leading in ministry, hundreds of hours clocked with my therapist, and the ability to share my "testimony" with ease, I reached my mid-thirties feeling more restless in my relationship with God and others than ever before; leery to approach either with absolute honesty. Attempts to dismiss my past left me defeated; simply praying about it kept me on a loop of self-preservation; and aligning myself with the recurring cheer that our "past does not define us" seemed out of line with the very nature of the God of the Bible.

With few Christian resources available on how to biblically connect where I've been with where I'm going, I decided to spend the next few years researching this restlessness for myself. *Nothing Wasted* is the culmination of what I discovered—how I stopped running from, blaming others for, and sugar-coating the cringe-worthiest parts of me. How I stopped rehearsing "what if" and "what would they think," and instead learned to trust a God with whom there are no accidents. A God who wants me, not in spite of my story but because of it.

This is my journey to finally believing God. I really hope it's yours too.

Thank you for taking a chance. I love you.

My friends call me,

Kase.

HOW TO GET THE MOST FROM THIS EXPERIENCE

Resources You'll Need

1. *Nothing Wasted* DVD or Digital Access (one per group)

Through live teaching, I personally walk you through each group session: challenging you, getting vulnerable with you, and connecting with you through time and distance in the supernatural love of God's Word. Each week's video session is approximately 20 minutes in length. If on your own, watch each week's video session and then journal through the discussion questions provided for you. If in a group, watch each session and openly discuss the questions together.

2. *Nothing Wasted Study Guide* (one per person)

The Bible study guide includes group discussion questions for participants after viewing each new session of video teaching. It also provides days of individual personal study exercises. Each day of personal study should take approximately 15–25 minutes.

3. Your own Bible

For both the group sessions and your individual study time, you will need a Bible you are comfortable reading. Don't stress about the translation—it doesn't have to be the same as mine or as the other people in your group. Just bring a Bible you feel drawn to and can understand easily. I primarily will be using the *New International Version* in the video session teaching and in the personal study. As a side note, some of my favorite and most used translations are the ESV, NIV, and NLT. If you don't have a Bible, get one! If cost is a factor, talk to people at your church and see if they can help you out.

4. Other resources

I recommend getting yourself a good Bible commentary. This will give you background and additional insights into the Scriptures and help you with tricky passages you may encounter. I have found *Logos Bible Software* to be helpful if you'd like an electronic option. Or, *Warren W. Wiersbe's Bible Exposition Commentary* is a favorite hardcover option.

5. *Nothing Wasted* book

The book was written to be read alongside this Bible study. Within the book I go deeper into my own story as well as my breaking point of surrender that ultimately led to God's grace-filled redemption, healing, and restoration of my life. The book will help especially if you are going through this study on you own. Because you won't be alone; you and I will be in the thick of it together.

The Group

- A small group can be as small as three or as big as thirteen. If you have a large group gathering for the video session, great! I encourage you to simply break up into smaller groups for discussion time.

- If you don't go to church and are not a part of a women's group, invite your coworkers, roommates, or moms from your kid's class, to join you!

- If possible, allow two hours of group time each week. This will allow adequate time for watching the video and discussing the questions.

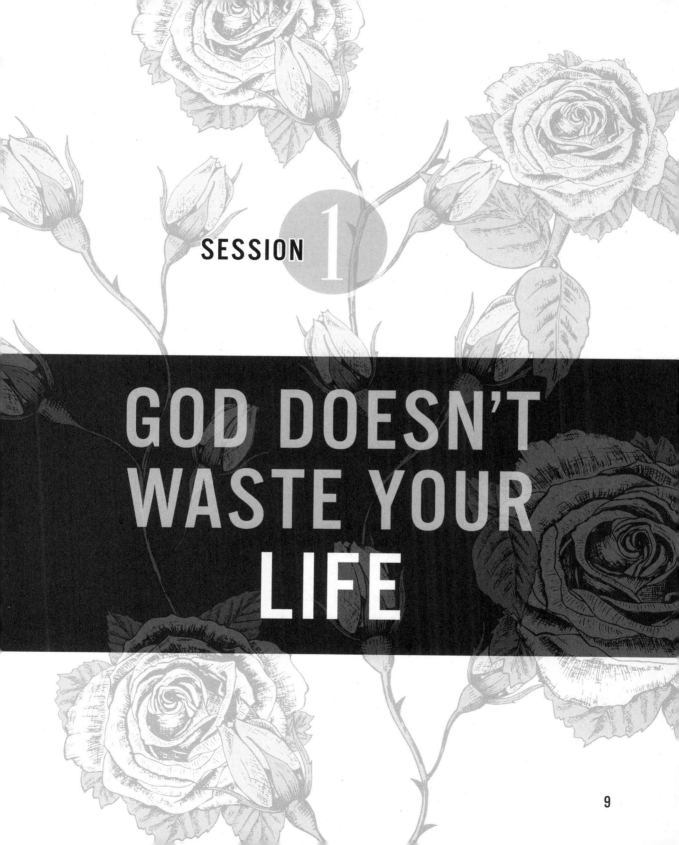

SESSION 1

GOD DOESN'T WASTE YOUR LIFE

This is a great week to read chapters 1–3 in the book!

Introduction (5 MINUTES)

Leader, please read aloud to group:

Predestined = {a course of events determined in advance by divine will}
  —Merriam Webster Dictionary

As humans, we tend to want to settle most matters of life in terms of "either-or." But with God, life is often "both-and." Although a "both-and" approach to destiny may not make sense to *our* mortal brain, we are underqualified for the job of universe-ruling. The good news is, *God* is powerful enough to hold together *both* his fixed plan for our life, while also honoring our free will to make decisions that influence our future.

The Bible teaches that while our choices *do* matter and influence the chain of events surrounding the whole of our life, they do not ultimately *determine* our future. This week we will learn that while God has given each of us the gift of free will, he also predestines our will to fit in the course of history he wants us to take. This view of God is a radical, theology-shifting, terrifyingly-liberating perspective, a perspective I sometimes regret I have experience enough to hold before you now. And yet I pray that, like me, you will never unsee the things we speak of here. That even in the midst of our greatest pain, doubt, and shame, we can confidently stake our claim in a God who says:

> **"Whatever I please, I do, in heaven and on
> earth, in the seas and all deeps."**
> **Psalm 135:6, my paraphrase**

> **"I work all things according to the counsel of my will."**
> **Ephesians 1:11, my paraphrase**

> "I am God, and there is no other; I am God, and there is none like me, declaring the end from the beginning and from ancient times things not yet done, saying, 'My counsel shall stand, and I will accomplish all my purpose.'"
>
> **Isaiah 46:9–10, my paraphrase**

Video Session 1 (18:30 MINUTES)

Watch Video Session 1 and fill in the blanks below.

1. It's not enough to say God *uses* our life if he does not also ___design___ it.

2. All of life's dismantling will eventually be seen for what it truly is: ___The good will of God___.

> "And we know that for those who love God all things work together for good, for those who are called according to his purpose."
>
> **Romans 8:28 ESV**

3. If we don't believe our life is designed and purposed by God, we will ___waste it___

4. God is using our ___location___, ___time in history___, ___parents___, ___experences___, to speak to us!

5. Never forget! This life is just one big ___set up___ by God!

6. God knows, the closer we are to him, the closer we are to ___who we are meant to be___.

7. When God asks us to ___obey___ him, he does so only from love, and always for our good.

NOW THAT'S GOOD . . .

Use this space to take notes of your own:

Group Discussion Questions (30 MINUTES)

Leader, read each question aloud to the group and encourage everyone to share.

1. What is your initial gut-reaction to the title of this Bible study: *Nothing Wasted: God Uses the Stuff You Wouldn't?* Why?   O. K. – Every Experience

2. If you were to describe how God orders events throughout history, what language would you choose? For example, "God permits . . ." "God orchestrates . . ." "God allows . . ." "God hopes . . ." Share your reasoning.

3. What does it mean for God to be "sovereign" (refer to Intro definition) over everything? What is liberating about this belief? What is difficult about this belief?   He will take care of us.

4. Look up and read Proverbs 16:1. As a group talk for a moment about this verse. What feelings, thoughts, questions does it evoke?

5. As you think about the whole of your life story thus far, to which statement do you most relate? "My story is too *rebellious* to be useful to God." Or, "My story is too *boring* to be useful to God." Share with the group why you chose your statement. (You don't have to be detailed in your response.)

SESSION 1 FOCUS   Bible Hub. com

God wastes no part of my story.
He has designed me on purpose, for purpose.

Closing Prayer

(lead out or ask for a volunteer)

Points of prayer for Session One:

- Conviction to complete the entire week of personal study.

- Supernatural energy and alertness to the way God is speaking to our hearts.

- Grace for the days we feel overwhelmed.

- Self-control to say "no" to good things and "yes" to best things.

- Patience to read and reread the Scripture prompts until our minds are clear with understanding.

GOD DOESN'T WASTE YOUR LIFE

Day 1
The Setup

This week my aim is to help you identify who God is to you *right now,* in light of who he's been to you in the past. My hope is that by the end of your devoted week of study, you will be just as convinced as I am that God has faithfully loved you all along; shaping, designing, and guiding the path of your entire life—good, bad, and ugly.

God's work in our lives does not begin the moment we are saved or at that one time of crisis we cried out to him because nothing else seemed to work. The shape of our entire lives was clear and useful to God long before we were born. Our parents, the neighborhood we grew up in, our skin color, financial situation, and point in human history, all thread together with our individual personality, style, and abilities, to bring maximum glory and honor to God's plan for eternity.

Our lives, including marriage and parenting as examples, are just one big setup to trust him more!

No one could have prepared me for how difficult marriage and parenting would be. Oh sure, I read books, attended conferences, and listened to the advice of those experienced in both. But advice could only take me so far. Not until I was a wife and mother for *myself* did I fully grasp the reality of responsibility those positions held. Even now, after twenty years of marriage and having children who are nearly teenagers, I feel as though each day is setting me up to trust God more quickly and frequently.

So is *life* for us all.

Life is one big leading question with God as the answer.

Day after day, God is setting us up to know him more, trust him more, and be satisfied by him more. Instead of recounting our seasons of pain, rebellion, and failure in self-loathing, bitterness, or anger, God gives us the grace to receive them as opportunity—an opportunity to believe God more naturally and more confidently than we did last time. Only in desperation and dependence will *his* nature bypass our requirements and become our reality.

Look up and read Matthew 16:13–17. Consider asking yourself the same question Jesus asks Peter in Matthew 16:15. How would you reply?

My Lord & Savior

According to this passage, **why** is Simon Peter **blessed** by his answer?

cause he knows him/Revelation

Although Jesus is asking the question in flesh-and-blood conversation, **whose** voice is Peter receiving access to **through** the presence of Jesus?

God

God, our Father, speaks no differently to us now than he did to Peter then. He speaks to our Spirit *through* Jesus, *for* Jesus. God uses language, tone, inflection, and narrative to tell us exactly how he feels about us and what his plan is for us. God speaks to us through words. But not just any words, *the* Word.

> "Long ago, at many times and in many ways, God spoke to our fathers by the prophets, but in these last days he has spoken to us by his Son, whom he appointed the heir of all things, through whom also he created the world."
> **Hebrews 1:1–2 ESV**

List three characteristics of the WORD God speaks to us based on John 1:1–14.

1. **John 1:2** *with God from the beginning*
2. **John 1:11** *His own did not receive him*
3. **John 1:14** *Word made flesh*

Whatever religious, comforting message wooed us in to the submission of belief and behavior, it will only lead to shame and condemnation without the words of Jesus as the *reality* of our heart. In other words, to hear from God, we must take personal *ownership* of our relationship with Jesus, not ride on the faithful coattails of others.

Is there an aspect of faith you embrace simply because someone else does it or because someone seemingly more intelligent than you said it? Example: going to church, doing this Bible study, a core belief, an opinion about someone else, serving on a committee, etc.?

_____

_____

_____

If Jesus is not our *personal* reality, then he is merely a spiritual pacifier; a good feeling when we show up for church; a great idea when life takes a nose-dive; a happy concept when we need to encourage someone in a dark place. But Jesus did not bleed and die to be a feeling, idea, or concept. He died to absorb every ounce of shame and condemnation we've felt over past sinful choices. And he rose to empower us to make a new, better choice for our future.

*"Yeah, yeah, Peter. I hear what everyone else is saying about me. But what about you? Who do **you** say that I am?"* (vs. 15, my paraphrase)

At the end of the day, when no one is looking, who is Jesus to *you*? If no other opinion mattered, if the score card and social media never existed, how often do you trust Jesus with your life . . . really?

Place a mark next to who Jesus is to you **right now** as your eyes meet this page . . .

_____ **The main character of the Bible.**

_____ **The reason why everything is happening.**

_____ **A good person who lived a good example of how to love others.**

_____ **A real relationship I am 100 percent committed to.**

√ **The only way I will truly hear the voice of God.** / *everything*

God wants us to take ownership of our faith. Therefore, he uses our life story to set us up for an honest, intimate relationship with him, a relationship so real and true that we communicate with him as a friend and seek wisdom from him as a father. God also wants to speak directly to us inside that reality, not as a mystical force or comforting concept, but as a *real relationship*. He will continue to ask us "who do you say I am?" through the people and experiences of our lives, *until* we believe his word for ourselves and, in turn, make decisions and take action from the ownership of that belief.

Please describe one way God is setting you up to believe him more right now. How does your current season of life reveal a need to trust God more today than you did yesterday? 8/11/20

Just our Journey from GA. to TN.

What is one area of your theology or core belief that you need to investigate more thoroughly? In other words, is there a particular subject of your faith you need to take ownership of? (i.e., what God says about premarital sex, how to pray, who to trust, political position, or your stance on homosexual relationships)

↑ All ↑

Day 2
Trust the Process

God's Word encourages us to remember our past. To think deeply about the experiences and people who have shaped us, and how they continue to influence our decisions in the present. He wants us to ask questions about the hard things, investigate the unexplainable things, get mad about the painful things, and celebrate the best things.

What he doesn't want? For us to get stuck on the thing itself as our identity.

He has no desire for a specific event or person to give meaning to our lives. Instead, he predetermines every event and person to impact our lives at the exact, right moment to see his meaning more clearly. *Moments*

> "I will remember the deeds of the LORD; yes,
> I will remember your wonders of old.
> I will ponder all your work, and meditate
> on your mighty deeds."
> **Psalm 77:11–12 ESV**

> "I will give thanks to the LORD with my whole heart;
> I will recount all of your wonderful deeds."
> **Psalm 9:1 ESV**

> "And those twelve stones, which they took out of the Jordan,
> Joshua set up at Gilgal. And he said to the people of Israel,
> 'When your children ask their fathers in times to come, "What
> do these stones mean?" then you shall let your children
> know, 'Israel passed over this Jordan on dry ground.'"'
> **Joshua 4:20–21 ESV**

remember what God did.

> "Remember the former things, those of long ago;
> I am God, and there is no other;
> I am God, and there is none like me."
>
> **Isaiah 46:9**

Slowing down long enough to remember how our past shapes our present, is critically important to our future relationship with God. Think for a moment about the important people in your life: a parent, boyfriend/girlfriend, child, best friend, or spouse. How did these particular people become special to you? In what way did they claim their position of priority in your life? That's right, over time.

It took time for you to get to know them, trust them, learn about them. Think about how methodically you studied your greatest romances. We can spend hours on the phone, infatuated with questions over someone we really care about. The same is true for our relationship with God. If we really want to know him, we must study him. And yes, of course, through the reading of his Word, but also through the specific ways he has shown that Word to be true over the course of our entire lives. *Yes*

Look up and read 2 Corinthians 3:18. Based on this verse, is trusting God in relationship a fast or slow process? _____

We can enjoy loads of freedom in the imagery that our relationship grows in God by "degree." Think of the slow shift in temperature from 70 to 71 degrees. Most people may not even notice the change. Perhaps *we* don't even realize the shift of atmosphere at first. But slowly, over time, we can look back and see the small, gradual moves from cold to hot faith in God.

If 10 degrees represents apathy and complacency in your relationship with God, and 100 degrees represents a burning passion to trust and obey God, place a mark on the degree of your relationship with God right now.

10 ——————— 30 ——————— 50 ——————— 70 ——————— 100

If you marked 50 or below, can you remember a time in your past when your love for God burned hotter? If so, describe what was going on at that time:

_____

_____

_____

If you marked 50 or above, what is currently going on in your life to help you raise the temperature of your desire to be in relationship with God?

_____

_____

_____

Read Ephesians 1:3–12 to answer the following questions (circle correct answer):

1. **At what point in time did we receive God's full blessing on our life?**

   The moment of our   Once we got our act   Before the founda-
   salvation   together   tions of the world

2. **God's purpose for our entire life first needed input from _____ to become a reality.**

   Us   Jesus   No one

3. **According to verse 11, how much of our life happens according to the predetermined will of God?**

   Some of it   Most of it   All of it

It's overwhelming. I get it. To believe God is in control over the good and happy moments of our life is one thing, but to trust he also had in mind all of the bad stuff too? It's a traumatizing consideration.

How could it be that God foreknew the evil of rape, and still let it happen? Or the devastation of poverty, racial discrimination, and addiction? How could God let someone be born to an absent or abusive father, or foresee a marriage that would end in divorce without sending flashing lights and signs to run the other direction?

According to verse 12, God's plan for our life is working out exactly the way he intends for one simple reason:

So that we can make sense of it	That we will feel better about our situation	To bring praise to Jesus

Nothing in the universe exists for its own sake. Everything exists to make the greatness of Christ more fully known—including you, the most annoying person you know, your worst day, and their worst day.

This truth changes everything for us. The concept of a sovereign God, governing both good and evil, ought to send a wave of emotion through your body, the consideration itself leading us to ask even more questions.

Good. It's time to start asking questions. It's time to investigate and dig for the absolute truth God is offering us in a world spinning on the axis of subjectivity.

How does it make you feel to consider God predetermines every person and event of your life? Is it liberating, maddening, confusing? Take a moment to write down your most honest thoughts:

Sovereignty

As we move forward in study, don't let go of the "degree" imagery. Remember, a solid relationship takes times to build. Trust must be established through consistency of presence in both the hills and valleys. Our world teaches us to get what we want when we want it. But with God, the process is the point.

Let yourself be free to consider your life as a journey, not an arrival. Slowly and intentionally, step by step, trust the process of God.

Day A Story to Be Told

God uses our mortal lifespan to slowly and intentionally transcend what we think we know about him, in order to give us a *true experience* of him. He uses one specific tool to accomplish this mission—a story.

Everyone's life is a story. And God clearly uses the art of storytelling as the language to stimulate the parts of us that are deeply connected to him.

Look up and read Ecclesiastes 3:11. According to this verse, what specific part of God are we designed to connect with?

Read 2 Samuel 12:1–15.

What parts of David's person are stimulated through Nathan's storytelling?

_____ **His mind**   _____ **His emotions**   _____ **His behavior**

Storylines not only connect us to one another, they create an opportunity for our nature to sync up to God's.

Storytelling is the oldest tool of influence in human history because it forces both the left and right side of our brain to work together—logic with creativity, facts with feelings, analysis with dreaming.

Read Exodus 6:1–8 for a *left-brain* experience.

Read Galatians 5:1 for a *right-brain* experience.

Both passages are saying the same thing in different ways. Now that both your left and right brain are working together, write the collaborative point of both passages?

Like eternity (Ecclesiastes 3:11), our desire to know and be known by others through the movement of story is deeply engrained in us. God created us with this desire, but also because he created his Son to be incredibly passionate about communicating through the art of storytelling.

Look up and read Matthew 13:34, then fill in the blanks.

All these things Jesus said to the crowds in _____; indeed, he said nothing to them without a _____.

Our life story allows us access to the grand narrative God is writing. But remembering our past is far from easy. Most of the messages we have heard over the course of our life evoke fear or shame when it comes to our past. Somewhere along the way we have believed the lie that our past does not define our present, and if it did, that would be a bad thing.

God tethers a pattern to our soul—a rhythm that our heart beats to without us realizing it—a loop that is replayed over and over throughout the course of the best and worst parts of our life. Redemption.

On pages 26–28 read each passage, answer the questions, and consider the related thought.

> "In the beginning, God created the heavens and the earth. The earth was without form and void, and darkness was over the face of the deep. And the Spirit of God was hovering over the face of the waters."
>
> **Genesis 1:1–2 ESV**

What seems to be the setting of this story? _____

Who do you think is the main character? _____

Consider: In the beginning, God; not in the beginning, us. What thoughts/feelings do you experience when you read that this world started for God and not for us?

_____

> "And God said, 'Let there be light,' and there was light."
>
> **Genesis 1:3**

What tells us something is about to happen here? _____

Consider: Despite the darkness we may feel, light is what happens when we engage the love of God and apply it to our past.

What are some of the darkest feelings or thoughts you experience when the lights are out?

_____

_____

_____

_____

> "Then God said, 'Let us make man in our image, after our likeness.'"
>
> **Genesis 1:26 ESV**

> "The Lord God took the man and put him in the garden of Eden to work it and keep it. And the Lord God commanded the man, saying, 'You may surely eat of every tree of the garden, but of the tree of the knowledge of good and evil you shall not eat, for in the day that you eat of it you shall surely die.'"
>
> **Genesis 2:15–17 ESV**

What is the "Rising Action" here? Rising action is the movement in a scene that makes you want to stick around to see what will happen next.

Consider: God creates his masterpiece, human beings, to reflect him and represent him on earth. In the garden, man and woman do not need God because they are sinful but simply because they are created beings—a result of intelligent design, not random mutation. Because God loves them so much, he wants to show them love though his promise of provision, blessing, abundant life, and the sweetest gift of all—the freedom in not being God.

Do you currently feel as though someone is constantly disappointing you or that you are disappointing someone? How would this relationship specifically change if you/they resigned yourselves to not be God?

> "I will put enmity between you and the woman, and between your offspring and her offspring; he shall bruise your head, and you shall bruise his heel."
>
> **Genesis 3:15 ESV**

The "Falling Action" of a story is oftentimes a hard, painful, or sad scene to watch, but it is also the movement leading toward a resolution. Describe what you think is happening here.

Consider: A new scene in God's story has just been introduced to the humans. The Director wrote the story from beginning to end long before "the beginning" credits. He knew that this would be the scene that changes everything. Enter: the hero—the "he" referred to above is Jesus. A rescue mission has commenced.

Where are you in this scene? Write a few words about your first encounter with Jesus and how exactly you feel that you need (or don't need) him to rescue you right now . . .

Day 4
Context Is Key

God knows his glory and holiness is too much for rebel humans to behold. Why? Because it changes us. His glory reminds us that we are dependent on something besides ourselves for life, love, and happiness. The realization that we are not God and incapable of saving people can paralyze us in doubt, shame, or fear. Therefore, God came to us in a form more palatable and identifiable to our frailty. He came as a human. He made himself one of us.

Jesus told more than thirty stories during his public ministry. Stories that help us think deeply. Stories that come through the back door of our preconceived notions, stereotypes, and defenses.

Stories such as the "Speck and the Log," warning us against the hypocrisy of judging another person. Or, the story of the "Lost Sheep," helping us understand the magnitude of God's love in his pursuit of a relationship with us.

An outline is a necessary first step to any good story. So, let's do that!

Think of one *descriptive* word for each *season of life* I have listed below. Your word does not need to be deep, profound, or even 100 percent accurate—just the first word you think of that would best describe that time as you remember it. I have given you an example from my life to help get you started.

NAME: *Kasey*

LIFE-STAGE (IN YEARS)	DESCRIPTIVE WORD
5 to 10	Confusing
11 to 14	Overwhelmed
15 to 18	Rebellious
19 to 25	Hard
26 to 30	Lowest Point
31 to 40	Reckoning
41 to 50	Redemptive

NAME: _____

LIFE-STAGE (IN YEARS)	DESCRIPTIVE WORD
5 to 10	
11 to 14	
15 to 18	
19 to 25	
26 to 30	
31 to 40	
41 to 50	
51 to 60	
61 to 70+	

Read Exodus 1:1–6. The children of Israel were originally from Canaan and descendants of who? _____

Who was Joseph? (Read Genesis 41:39–45) _____

Why did the descendants of Joseph travel to Egypt? (Read Genesis 41:56–57)

_____

The Israelite people were originally welcomed into Egypt under the watchful eye of Joseph, but many years had passed, and the new king of Egypt was not a fan.

Why was the new king so intimidated? (Read Exodus 1:8) _____

Apparently, Egypt was a great place to live under Joseph's rule, because the Israelites never returned to their homeland of Canaan. Instead, they settled in, found work, got married, and had babies—lots and lots of babies.

What orders were given by the king when his fear of being overthrown by the Israelites consumed him? (Read Exodus 1:15–16) _____

But what happened instead? (Read Exodus 1:17) _____

At this time, Hebrew women could have easily been assimilated into the Egyptian population. Females would have been integrated into the Egyptian families through marriage, as concubines, or as servants. Yet, the large number of men made it impossible for the Egyptians to achieve the one-world domination and government they desired. So, the king gave orders to kill all the male Hebrew babies.

Can you imagine the length of creativity a mother would be willing to go in such desperate times as this?

What did Jochebed do to save the life of her son? (Read Exodus 2:1–4) _____

_____

Who found Jochebed's son? (Read Exodus 2:5–6) _____

Now this is God's redemptive artistry at its finest!

As you may remember, Moses went on to lead the massive population of Israelites out of their Egyptian oppression. But he, and he alone, would be the only one qualified to lead such an exodus.

Here's the setup:

For the first five to eight years of Moses' life he was raised by his own family! This development allowed him access to his identity, heritage, his biological parents, and genetic predeterminants.

If Moses had not been raised by his own family, he would have lacked a racial identity, which would veto him from the trust of the Israelites when it came time to lead them out of their slavery.

In his teens and young adulthood, Moses lived as an Egyptian. He received an education, training, and the respect he would have never received as a poor Hebrew slave. Moses could have never been the deliverer of his people unless identifying with both people groups—Israelite and Egyptian.

Not only was Moses' identity a blend, his feelings and behaviors were a mix too. You can see his struggle in what happens next. Read Exodus 2:11–15.

Moses' life could no longer bear the weight of existing as both a prince of Egypt and a prince of Israel. When the decision to choose one or the other was finally upon him, he panicked—in his anger, confusion, and anxiety, Moses killed an Egyptian taskmaster, which was no biggie to the Egyptian authorities. Moses didn't run because he feared punishment for his crime (it was common for a leader to kill a slave if he wanted to). Moses ran because he was not at home—born of God's chosen people, yet living as a pagan, makes for one epic identity crisis.

Moses also had a temper that needed to be dealt with. He was arrogant and prideful. He had the heart of an Israelite but the habits and defenses of an Egyptian.

By the time Moses met the shepherdess of his dreams, he'd been roaming around in the wilderness forty years! Doubtful Moses realized that his forty years of shepherding sheep were preparing him for another forty years of shepherding people.

All of this context is key. Puzzle-piecing the seasons of Moses' life together like this points to the proof of God's hand in all of it! The same is true for us.

God had Moses in training. As a shepherd in the wilderness, Moses was learning to be responsive to the Spirit, aware of his anger and pride, learning the patience required to protect and care for a flock of unruly animals, and understanding what it feels like to be totally dependent on God.

As you consider how important the context/story of your past is to your present, are specific insecurities and/or fears beginning to surface? If so, please describe some of what you are feeling.

Day 5
Planned on Purpose

Our story is truer than any other reality we know, and each of us must discover the meaning of what God has written as our life story.

As a child, Moses could have been driven by his desire to earn the approval of his parents. As a teenager, he may have been motivated by the platform and power of the

Egyptian throne. We know that as a young man, he was driven by a desire for justice with a sprinkling of pride, anger, and fear.

But as an old man, after considerable time spent thinking about his life and listening to the right voice, Moses was driven by only one thing—deliverance.

Perhaps it's time we consider what internal force might be driving our life.

Place a number (1–10) in the blank next to the statement as it most honestly applies to you right now.

1 = never feel this way, 5 = sometimes feel this way, 10 = always feel this way

STATEMENT 1

_____ I feel as though there are secret places in me that if I were to openly share would cause people to leave me or treat me differently.

STATEMENT 2

_____ I do not feel comfortable receiving love from others without giving them something in return. I am often worried about what other people think of me and will change my mood, tone of voice, or behavior to fit their desired perception of me.

STATEMENT 3

_____ I think through every angle of an opportunity to the point that I forget why I wanted it in the first place. I appreciate controlled environments that lend themselves to a result I am comfortable with.

STATEMENT 4

_____ I think and/or talk about a painful event from my past often. I feel helpless to change things that haunt me.

STATEMENT 5

_____ I want to enjoy life more than I do right now, and I am willing to do whatever it takes to get there. I don't hesitate to put an expense on the credit card if there is not enough money in my bank account.

Take a look back at your numbers.

Each statement describes a significant motivation of a person's heart—the mind-set that can drive us in daily decision-making. The higher your number, the higher the likelihood you are functioning from this place; or at least, have the tendency to go there more frequently than the others—especially during times of high stress, life-transitions, relational strife, or conflict.

Statement 1: **Guilt-driven**

Statement 2: **Approval-driven**

Statement 3: **Fear-driven**

Statement 4: **Resentment-driven**

Statement 5: **Material-driven**

Which motivation was your highest number? _____

Was there a tie between two? _____

Which motivation was your lowest? _____

How does this inventory make you feel? Do you agree or disagree? _____

_____

If you agree, can you identify an event or person in your past that you attach this motivation to? If so, please write it here: _____

_____

Like Moses, where our human motivations and mind-sets push us into static inertia, the love of God bids us to move.

For example, if Pharaoh had not attempted to kill the Hebrew baby boys in Egypt, Moses would have never had his unique background that made him a champion capable of leading an oppressed people out of a major world power. Not only that, if Moses had not totally blown it by killing a man, he would have never spent those 40 years in the wilderness to identify himself as a child of the God of his forefathers. Moses needed that time in the wilderness to remember—to slow down defenses, think about his motives, be deeply self-aware of his sin and grief, and to finally be at peace with a storyline that even he could not mess up.

God is weaving together the impossible, wonderful scenes of our life story to point us to the best story ever told—Jesus loves *all* of you. Not in spite of you, because of you.

Perhaps you are young and struggling with quick, selfish responses. Maybe you are middle-aged and finding yourself smack dab in wilderness training. Or perhaps you are seasoned, steady, and fully-prepared to walk back into Egypt to set the captives free.

Wherever you are on this journey, trust the voice of God, the process of God, and the story God is telling with your life.

No detail has been left to chance. No circumstance is random. No hardship wasted.

No part of your life is wasted by God. But instead, useful to bring his Son glory.

"For you created my inmost being;
      you knit me together in my mother's womb.

"I praise you because I am fearfully and wonderfully made;
      your works are wonderful,
      I know that full well.

"My frame was not hidden from you
      when I was made in the secret place,
      when I was woven together in the depths of the earth.

"Your eyes saw my unformed body;
      all the days ordained for me were written in your book
      before one of them came to be."

Psalm 139:13–16

SESSION 2

GOD DOESN'T WASTE YOUR RELATIONSHIPS

This is a great week to read chapters 4–7 in the book!

Introduction (5 MINUTES)

Leader, please read aloud to group:

First Corinthians 1:9 reminds us that "God's faithfulness has called us into the fellowship of his Son" (my paraphrase). This "fellowship" is the mutual bond of Jesus that all Christians share, positioning us in a deep, eternal relationship with one another. This promise (and command) is the glorious news that we must not live one more minute believing the lie that we are alone in this life.

Please spend this week fighting any tendency to distrust God on the subject matter of relationships; choose instead to believe that God will never set us up for failure when it comes to our relationships. Isolation in and of itself is not compatible with the nature of God. Loneliness is not a biblical design, and "doing it yourself" is heresy.

God is using exactly who we are, surrounded by the exact people we are, to knock the props out from under our heart so that we will fully rely on him. This is the aim of God in all our pain and loss—whether received by our parents, friends, or brought on ourselves.

Whoever you are right now, wherever you're getting it right or wrong in relationships, and to whomever lovely or unlovely parents you were born, you are exactly where you are meant to be to receive God's ultimate healing.

> **"A friend loves at all times, and a brother**
> **is born for a time of adversity."**
> **Proverbs 17:17**

"In anger his master handed him over to the jailers to be tortured, until he should pay back all he owed. This is how my heavenly Father will treat each of you unless you forgive your brother or sister from your heart."

Matthew 18:34–35

"And everyone who has left houses or brothers or sisters or father or mother or wife or children or fields for my sake will receive a hundred times as much and will inherit eternal life."

Matthew 19:29

"If anyone does not know how to manage his own family, how can he take care of God's church?"

1 Timothy 3:5

"Both the one who makes people holy and those who are made holy are of the same family. So Jesus is not ashamed to call them brothers and sisters."

Hebrews 2:11

Video Session 2 (25:30 MINUTES)

Watch Video Session 2 and fill in the blanks below.

1. We are made to delight in a _____, intimate God.

2. We cannot grow in the image of God without _____.

> **"See to it, brothers and sisters, that none of you has a sinful, unbelieving heart that turns away from the living God. But encourage one another daily, as long as it is called 'Today,' so that none of you may be hardened by sin's deceitfulness."**
> **Hebrews 3:12–13**

3. It's one thing to believe in God, but a much different thing to _____ him.

4. God refers to any of our unprocessed pain as a _____.

5. We know we are struggling to love fully, if we are _____

6. Our greatest fear is that we will be _____

> **"I will give you a new heart and put a new spirit in you; I will remove from you your heart of stone and give you a heart of flesh."**
> **Ezekiel 36:26**

7. What do we desperately need in relationships? A _____

8. God can extend his _____ without needing anything from us in return.

AMEN TO THAT!

Use this space to take notes of your own:

_____

_____

_____

_____

_____

Group Discussion Questions (30 MINUTES)

1. What quality do you value most in a friendship and why?

2. Can you name at least three people of the same gender who have been in your life on a consistent basis for the past three years? If yes, what specific things do you do to stay intentional with these friendships? If not, why?

3. Think of one of the most difficult people from your past, a person who singlehandedly changed the way you would go on to engage future relationships. Do feelings around this person still emerge when attempting to make new friendships or keep old ones? If yes, why do you think so?

4. At what point do you think relational wounds heal? In other words, what would be the *present* evidence in a person's life that *past* rejection, betrayal, abuse, or loss no longer holds them back from trusting God's plan for their life?

5. Why do you think God chose relationships and community as the best way to show his love to us?

SESSION 2 FOCUS:

God wastes no relationship.
He uses each one to prove he is the only one always with us and for us.

Closing Prayer

(lead out or ask a volunteer)

Points of prayer for Session Two:

- A calm mind and body as we revisit old pain.

- Humility instead of resentment wherever unresolved relationships surface.

- Clear focus on the goal of this week—releasing others from our expectations in order to trust God more fully.

- Courage to stay the course of the entire week of study despite what feelings or thoughts seek to distract us.

- An open mind to the possibility that God is ready to do the impossible.

PERSONAL BIBLE STUDY Session 2

GOD DOESN'T WASTE YOUR RELATIONSHIPS

Day 1

Weak Eyes

Look up and read Genesis 29:16–30, noting particularly the description of Leah versus that of Rachel in verse 17.

"Weak eyes" translates = {soft, homely, droopy, bulging, crooked, or fragile}

Based on your experience as a woman, do you think Leah struggled with insecurity in her physical appearance? What is a likely statement she played on repeat in her mind about the way she looked?

_____

_____

_____

As Rachel's older sister, what right in marriage did Leah have according to the custom and time (vs. 26)?

_____

_____

What internal dialogue do you think Leah was having with herself when Jacob desired to break the cultural norm and choose Rachel for his wife instead of her?

_____

_____

_____

_____

After seven years of watching Jacob fall in love with her younger sister, what emotions and thoughts do you think Leah held back as she lay there having sex with Jacob, knowing the he wished she were someone else.

_____

_____

_____

To feel chosen, seen, and accepted is a rush to the senses; a glorious hope that we are not as unloved or unwanted as we originally thought.

Describe your first memory of being chosen in a way that communicated acceptance to every part of you—mind, body, and soul. *This might look like unwavering love from your parents, your first kiss, a kind college roommate, or your "I do." I am searching for the moment you were* **consciously** *aware that, while rejection was an option, you instead, were chosen.*

_____

_____

_____

_____

Do you have a specific person or memory that comes to mind when you think about **not** being accepted? Please carefully and slowly ponder the following questions as you answer them in first person:

_____

_____

_____

_____

- As a **child**, I felt **chosen**. On my worst days and their worst days, I never doubted my parents (caretakers) wanted me. **TRUE / FALSE**

- As a **child**, I felt **safe** at home. I knew I could be my most honest self and still be accepted. **TRUE / FALSE**

- As a **teenager**, I struggled with the fear of rejection:

  _____ **Normally (like everyone else hitting puberty)**
  _____ **Intensely (more than most)**
  _____ **Obsessively (all I thought about, dictated most of my life choices)**

- I can remember a time when I was rejected because of the way I looked. **TRUE / FALSE**

- I can remember a time when I was rejected because another person was more preferred than me. **TRUE / FALSE**

- I relate to **Leah** in the following way(s):

  _____

  _____

  _____

Of all the wounds that attach themselves to us most deeply, *rejection* is perhaps the most painful. Unlike uncontrollable circumstances, like death or relocation, rejection carries the sting of choice. Rejection is *not* uncontrollable. Rejection is the choice *not* to accept.

Sometimes, choosing to take a break or end a relationship is valid and necessary.

Name one reason why *ending* a relationship would be more beneficial than continuing on with it?

_____

_____

But most often, denying a person full access to our love and resources is the unnecessary, easy excuse, in an effort to hide our own insecurities. And because rejection is not simply an emotion we feel, it is capable of sending a message to the core of our identity—a message that shapes the way we engage others, ourselves, and God.

This week, consider how rejection has shaped/is shaping your relationships with others, but most importantly, your relationship with God. Undealt with, festering rejection from our past seeks to steal the crown of God's authority and lordship over our lives. If we allow it, the lie that we are not accepted can become the guiding force for our lives, talking us in to thoughts, words, and behaviors radically different from the person we know we are.

Undealt with, rejection also paralyzes our desire to seek out things such as reconciliation, forgiveness, honesty, and intimacy—all important marks of a maturing Christian faith.

Ask the Lord to prepare your heart to believe this truth in the place of any unresolved fear still lurking within you:

> **"Once you were alienated from God and were enemies in your minds because of your evil behavior. But now he has reconciled you by Christ's physical body through death to present you holy in his sight, without blemish and free from accusation."**
> **Colossians 1:21–22**

Day 2
Seen and Heard

Read Genesis 29:31–35. Based on verse 31, was the rejection Leah felt "all in her head," or did someone else agree with her? What happened to confirm this?

_____

_____

_____

What sense of God did Leah attribute to the birth of her first son, Reuben? (vs. 32)

_____

What sense of God did Leah attribute to the birth of her second son, Simeon? (vs. 33)

_____

Based on what you read in this passage, either explicit or implicit, what specific response did Leah want from her husband (Jacob) through the births of these three children:

⬤ Birth of Reuben = _____

⬤ Birth of Simeon = _____

⬤ Birth of Levi = _____

As we engage the topic of rejection, is there an old soul wound resurfacing within you? Soul wounds can resurface as either **healed** or **harmful**.

A healed soul wound can still hurt but no longer motivates our need. However, harmful soul wounds continue to navigate for us. This unresolved pain still has a say in the way we relate to others, specifically in regard to how much we *need* from others.

Example of a HEALED soul wound in your life:

Example (if any) of a HARMFUL soul wound in your life:

After reading Leah's story, do you find yourself a bit protective of her?

As women, I think we get her.

Some of us *have* been someone's *second* choice. And we *all* have physical imperfections that bother us and tempt us to feel like the "ugly duckling" in a room full of swans.

In short, we all know rejection.

Did you notice the two *senses* Leah attributed to the Lord after the birth of her two sons? "*The L ORD **looked** on her affliction,*" and "***heard*** *that* [*she*] *was hated*" (ESV).

Don't you know Leah wanted to shake Jacob and scream; "I can be a good wife to you! Look at all these babies I've given you! I know I'm not pretty like Rachel, but I'm loyal, honest, and nurturing. Just love me and see!"

Based on verses 33 and 34, what are the two things Leah wants as a result of her childbirths, and *who* does she want them from?

_____

_____

_____

Is there someone in your life whom you wish would *see* and *hear* you better? Describe that person's relevancy to your life and why their acknowledgment of you is important.

_____

_____

_____

_____

What specifically, in your behavior or words, gets misunderstood most often by this person?

_____

_____

_____

Write one specific thought or behavior that might change in your life if you *no longer needed* this particular person to see/hear/understand you?

_____

_____

No matter how much we want to be seen and heard by other people, even the people who *should* see and hear us, "in the morning," they will always be Leah.

Look up and read Genesis 29:22–25.

Leah represents all the things and people who show their true colors in the light of day. Her life is an example that no matter how desperately we long for a particular friendship, marriage, child, career, or experience to satisfy us, we will always be left wanting. Whatever feels unseen or unheard in our hearts right now will never be fully understood by the subjective and collective opinion of people.

Leah's story may not be one of reconciled relationships or a well-deserved acknowledgment from her husband, but she did seem to find the acceptance and love she'd always longed for.

According to Genesis 29:35, *"[Leah] conceived again, and when she gave birth to a son she said, 'This time I will praise the Lord.' So she named him Judah. Then she stopped having children."*

By the arrival of her fourth son, Leah seemed to understand what so many of us miss through the heartbreaking pain of rejection—*God is the only one who truly accepts us.*

Leah received peace in the midst of rejection through one small shift in perspective—*"this time, she praised the Lord."*

Yes, she was a victim. No, she was not the first choice. No, time did not heal old wounds. The pain of her reality could have suffocated her in bitterness the rest of her life, but instead she allowed her broken relationships to lead her into believing a God who saw her, heard her, and wanted her.

Finally, his love was enough.

Day 3
Been There, Done That

The enemy's voice is loudest in the midst of rejection.

As it was for Leah, so it can be for us—the more rejected we feel, the harder we work to prove ourselves worthy; hustling, busy, over-compensating, over-thinking, and over-expecting.

This is right where Satan wants us—trading love as a commodity instead of giving and receiving love in grace.

But, when we remember the incredible lengths Jesus has gone for us; when we acknowledge his undeserved rejection on our behalf, and God's desire to use "what is low and despised in the world, even things that are not, to bring to nothing things that are" (1 Corinthians 1:28 ESV), we no longer need our worth assigned or defined by people.

According to Isaiah 53:2–4:

● Was Jesus average or handsome in his appearance?

● What did men think of him?

● Because of man's rejection, what specific feeling was Jesus acquainted with?

- What specific behavior did Jesus endure at the hands of men (vs. 3a)?

- Was he popular and well-liked according to end of verse 3?

- What two things does Jesus carry for us (vs. 4)?

Jesus didn't just feel rejected, he *was* rejection.

There will never be a time in our life when we will experience even half the rejection, betrayal, and un-chosen-ness that Jesus did on our behalf.

According to 1 Peter 2:

- Verse 24: Where did Jesus personally carry our pain and sin?

- Verse 4: Why was Jesus **chosen** to do this for us?

- Verse 5: Are we meant to be like or unlike him?

- Verse 7: What is the sign that we believe Jesus is God's chosen Son?

● Verse 8: What is the sign that we do **not** believe Jesus is God's chosen Son?

_____

God does not demand our trust. He proves his faithfulness from the other side.

At great cost and grief, God sent his only Son to be rejected, suffer devastating pain at the hands of mortal men, and bleed his own blood through a brutal, horrific, unjust death. Because Jesus went the _full_ way, we have _a_ way—a way through the horribly painful experience of being rejected.

Describe a personal experience that connects you to the unjust rejection of Jesus—a time when someone turned their back on you, disliked you, or distanced themselves from you, when you did nothing wrong.

_____

_____

_____

_____

Does this wound still bother you? If yes, describe a few feelings that resurface when you think about being rejected this way. If no, describe the thoughts/behaviors you attended to in order to be free of lingering anxiety/doubt surrounding the rejection.

_____

_____

_____

_____

Leah got her life back when she believed where God had already been.

As she believed her full acceptance in God, Leah no longer needed the acceptance of others, not even from those called to be responsible for accepting her.

Jesus has been there, done that. Through *his* rejection, *we are* **accepted**.

Accepted into what, you may be asking. "*. . . a chosen race, a royal priesthood, a holy nation, a people for his own possession, that you may proclaim the excellencies of him who called you out of darkness into his marvelous light.*" (1 Peter 2:9 ESV)

Day
View from the Top

Offense = {Annoyance or resentment brought about by a perceived insult to or disregard for oneself or one's standards or principles.}

Based on this definition, use the following scale to honestly mark where you fall on most days.

1	3	5	7	9
Never offended	Rarely offended	Sometimes offended	Often offended	Bitter about life in general

Our inclination toward being offended is a strong sign of how deep and unresolved our wound of rejection is.

The truth is, any message, regardless of right or wrong motivation, has the potential to offend us.

How often and easily we "get our feelings hurt" is an indicator of how much or how little healing we have received to our old, internal wound of rejection.

To the degree we have allowed God to heal our past wound of rejection is the degree we presently absorb offense.

When was the last time you remember feeling offended? Describe what happened.

_____

_____

_____

How would your day (thoughts, behaviors, facial expressions) have looked differently had you chosen *not* to be offended (despite the right or wrong intention of the other)?

_____

_____

_____

What is the core message in offense for you? In other words, what is the real issue motivating you toward offense? An unspoken, old wound of rejection, perhaps?

_____

_____

_____

Jesus calls and equips us for a *higher* response to what offends us. First, he tells us the truth—we are finally and fully **accepted** in him. And through that truth, we have "received everything we need for a godly life" (2 Peter 1:3), in order that we might "bear with each other and forgive one another if any of you has a grievance against someone" (Colossians 3:13).

Write Proverbs 10:12 in the space below:

Often, the person we push out or back away from is the same person we hold to a higher expectation than others. In short, we tend to "hate" the ones we hope will love us most.

Our choice to be satisfied in God means we no longer "need" other people to fill our gaps. From this posture, we are armed with more than enough blanket to *cover* over the most painful wounds and offenses.

When our relationship in God is enough, we will restrain our urge to "stir up drama" in other relationships, avoiding extreme emotions like hate.

Who is someone you love so much that receiving offenses from them turns quickly to extremes, such as strife (arguments) and hate (extreme dislike)?

What is one expectation you have for this person that you could let go of today and still be satisfied in God?

What is one way that you will choose to place a blanket/covering of love over this relationship?

_____

_____

Only with a blanket of God's love over our own heart will we have enough security to seek the best for another person in the midst of their worst. First, we must believe our supernatural ability to not only dismiss an offense, but completely cover it. If we are truly after love, we have the strength to absorb all kinds of hurtful words and behaviors. We know that we are in the business of "covering," when we:

- Do not bring up the offense in conversation with others,

- Continue to engage the offender in the same way we did prior to the offense,

- Engage the offender with the healthy, life-giving behaviors we would like in return.

Secondly, we must be willing to stop a repetitious behavior or pattern of speech that is causing tension or division in the relationship.

Perhaps the motive behind our word or action is not inherently wrong or intended to wound. Perhaps you are not even thinking about what you are doing or saying because it would not be personally "offensive" to you. Regardless of our intention, choosing to repeat an offense after it is clearly harmful or divisive will bring a painful end to the relationships meant to secure us to the love of God.

Think back on the past few years of your friendships. Do you have 1–2 friends that have stuck with you through thick and thin? If yes, how do you intentionally seek love for them? If no, are you able to identify a specific, repeated pattern of behavior that might be pushing potentially good friends away?

_____

_____

_____

_____

_____

Write Proverbs 19:11 in the space below:

_____

_____

Notice from this verse, in order to "overlook an offense" you must first slow down your anger. In other words, take a breath when that defensive default sends a heat wave over your body. You know, the emotionally-charged feeling you get whenever you feel you're second choice, misunderstood, falsely accused, unseen, unheard, manipulated, or used.

Overlook = {to view from above}

In the blow of any offense, true or false, our "good sense" (wisdom gained from past experience) ought to remind us to reign in our emotions until we can _see above_ the issue.

To "overlook" does not mean to "excuse" or "avoid." But instead, to consider the full context to the best of our ability—to rise _above_ the feeling of offense, investigate both sides, and _then_ decide if the matter is worth withdrawal, knots in our stomach, or walking away.

Our glory is God's glory. And he is most glorified when we are most satisfied in him.

Try to see things from your friend's vantage point. Think of how they might be hurting in every situation. Even if you don't agree with their stance or their reaction, find a way to identify with their hurt, just as Christ did for you.

You don't have to validate a person's actions to identify with their hurt. People are exhausting, careless, and constantly disappointing us. This is God's design. God is using unqualified human love to constantly remind us how desperate we are for him—the only love who will truly accept us right where we are, at all times, no strings attached.

Day 5
Relationship Rescue

While God's voice is discerned intimately and differently within each one of us, it always aligns with his perfect will. He will never ever act outside of his perfect good nature. Therefore, no part of you or your life experience has fallen away from the center of his sovereignty. We are exactly where we are meant to be, at exactly the right time, with exactly the right people.

Even our reckless days of rebellion and long winters of waiting are being used by God to bring himself glory and secure us to his love. Which means, our hardest hits with rejection are also our greatest opportunities to rescue the potential of our relationships.

1. REJECTION REVEALS

Rejection surfaces what is most important to us.

If we want something bad enough, we are willing to wade through miles of criticism and hurt feelings to get it. God wants us to feel this way about him. Jesus felt this way about us—willing to be rejected as an innocent man because he thought us worth the cost. If we are not willing to do the same for him, perhaps we do not want him badly enough.

Are you willing to fight for your faith, your spouse, your child, or those less fortunate, even if it costs your reputation, time, or resources? Write down a situation or person you are committing to fight harder for as you close this week of study.

2. REJECTION RESCUES

There is a big difference between rejection and correction. When done right and well, giving or receiving correction brings a relationship closer not further apart.

One redemptive use of rejection is its purpose of rescuing a relationship that is on the verge of destruction. Matthew 18:15 refers to it as winning your brother over.

We know it's time for someone to say hard things whenever a person's sin or unhealthy behavior is serious enough to cool down or rupture the relationship. Differences of opinion, personality, style, or way of engagement are not and should not be reason enough to confront someone.

In addition, we must not confront unless we are also willing to carry. Galatians 6:1–2 reminds us that correction offers help carrying the burden of the other with a gentle and spiritual hand. A healthy confrontation will always offer ideas on how both parties can work out the issue together.

Rescue motivates loving correction.

The more rejection we have personally experienced, the more willing we will be to accept the apologies we get without demanding people to admit more than they honestly believe.

Is there a conflict or tense relationship in your life in need of rescue? If so, write a few ways you can correct in a way that honors this particular relationship. What way of gentleness and burden-bearing would this person appreciate from you? (Think, their "love language," not yours).

_____

_____

_____

_____

Answer the following questions based on Galatians 5:13–15, 5:24–6:3.

1. According to verse 13, what are we created for?

_____

2. How do we compromise this calling?

_____

On the other hand, how do we maintain security in this position? (vs. 13)

_____

3. What is the one statement summing up both the Old and New Testaments? (vs. 14)

_____

4. What do you think it means to "bite" and "devour" one another? (vs. 15)

_____

5. According to verse 24, the only way to kill off the desires destroying our relationships is to _____ to God.

6. Verse 26 warns of three ways we destroy relationships:

- ○ _____
- ○ _____
- ○ _____

If a friend truly is in the wrong, Galatians 6:1 tells us to approach them in what way?

_____

Although our friend may be wrong, does that mean we are incapable of the same wrong? _____ (vs. 1)

Circle the correct answer based on 6:2. We fulfill the entire mission of Jesus when we:

- ○ Point out another's problems.
- ○ Give money to another's problems.
- ○ Talk to someone else about another's problems.
- ○ Bear the weight of another's problem alongside them.
- ○ Walk in front of another's problems as the example.

What is one way we break the line of trust and intimacy within ourselves, therefore with God? (vs. 3)

_____

3. REJECTION REDIRECTS

God doesn't just see our lives from where we are—he sees our lives in eternal perspective; how the beginning and end of our time on earth will matter to our time in heaven. Perhaps you have lived long enough to affirm Garth Brooks' famous lyric as truth: "Sometimes I thank God for unanswered prayers." If not, it won't be long until you do.

> **"There is a way that seems right to a man,**
> **but its end is the way to death."**
> **Proverbs 14:12 ESV**

Rejection is redeemed by God as he uses it to redirect us from something we think we want onto something we really need. God's way is always good, regardless of how it feels coming at us. His plan for us produces fruit, gives life, and duplicates his goodness in every relationship we encounter.

You may be holding a heartbreaking loss in your hands—loss of an important relationship, position, dream, or reputation. The question is not, does it hurt? The question is, where is it taking you?

Rejection can either break or build your relationships with others. And most importantly, with God. But Jesus hung on the cross to build a bridge of acceptance between us and God. The "stone the builders rejected, has become the cornerstone" (Matthew 21:42). Meaning, from our **accepted** position in Christ, rejection cannot, will not, break us. It may exhaust us, discourage us, or put an end to seasons and relationships we "wish" for us, but rejection will never destroy us.

What rejections from your past are being used to strengthen you for future relationships? Please list those you have lived long enough to see God redeem, as well as those you are believing him to redeem in the future.

_____

_____

_____

_____

_____

SESSION 3

GOD DOESN'T WASTE YOUR REGRET

This is a great week to read chapters 8–10 in the book!

Introduction (5 MINUTES)

Leader, please read aloud to group:

Regret = {to feel sad, repentant, or disappointed over something that has happened or been done, especially a loss or missed opportunity}

We all have things we've said or done that we wish we could do over. What would you go back and change if you could? Would you say no to that first drink or be a better parent to your children? Would you refuse to click on that website or walk away from the gossip?

We must all live with the harm we've done to others or that's been done to us. There is no redo/undo button to life. But there is a reality of hope we can embrace in light of our regret—the hope that God *purposes* our most painful choices and offers deliverance from our desire to live in slavery to those choices.

Giving ourselves permission to remember and share the most painful, stupid, or embarrassing things we've done (or that have been done *to us*), is the first step toward healing any unresolved hurt that may be the culprit behind consistent patterns of dysfunctional behavior or shallow self-awareness.

Psalm 32:3 tells us that when "we keep silent about our sin, it feels as though our bones are wasting away" (my paraphrase). So, the first step in dealing with our regret is to have it. Feel it. Admit it. Don't hide it. Say it right to God's face, just as David did in the psalm:

> "Then I acknowledged my sin to you and did not cover up my iniquity.
> I said, 'I will confess my transgressions to the LORD.'
> And you forgave the guilt of my sin."
>
> **Psalm 32:5**

The hope of this week of study is to give you a moment in time to inhale and exhale the Holy Spirit as the full measure of approval and consent to relive the most embarrassing or painful memories of your past, alongside a loving Father who will never use your honesty against you.

> **The saying is trustworthy and deserving of full acceptance, that
> Christ Jesus came into the world to save sinners, of whom I am
> the foremost. But I received mercy for this reason, that in me, as
> the foremost, Jesus Christ might display his perfect patience as
> an example to those who were to believe in him for eternal life.**
>
> **1 Timothy 1:15–16 ESV**

Video Session Three (19 MINUTES)

Watch Video Session 3 and fill in the blanks below.

1. Once our _____ rests in God, our sinful behaviors eventually work themselves out.

> **"The LORD does not look at the things people look at. People look
> at the outward appearance, but the LORD looks at the heart."**
>
> **1 Samuel 16:7**

2. Our greatest regret and rebellion find their beginning in four words: _____

_____ ?

3. We are free _____ to be God.

4. The _____ of Jesus ruins us for the things that live in the _____ .

5. Only in the place of our _____ will our _____ be restored.

6. We wouldn't know our _____ were so weak if we hadn't tested them out in the first place.

7. God gives us over to our sin that we may finally be _____ .

PREACH . . .

Use this space to take notes of your own:

_____

_____

_____

_____

_____

_____

_____

_____

_____

_____

_____

Group Discussion Questions (30 MINUTES)

1. Romans 14:23 tells us that "*anything that does not come from faith is sin.*" Take a moment to discuss the implications of this verse. How does this verse convict your own heart and/or help you see people differently who are obviously living in sin?

2. What would you say to someone who says they have no regrets? Do you think it is possible to have no regrets? Why or why not?

3. How might God use our sinful choices (or another's sinful choices toward us) to empower us with a greater sense of grace, gratitude, and joy?

4. Share a past painful/embarrassing moment that has been redeemed and how the experience has been useful.

SESSION 3 FOCUS

God doesn't waste our regret.

Instead, he helps us repent and forgive so that regret can never be used against us.

Closing Prayer

(lead out or ask a volunteer)

Points of prayer for Session Three:

● Courage to trust God with every inch of our past.

● Humility to fight the lie of big versus small sins.

● Patience with ourselves as we dig in to places our pride desperately hates to expose.

● A recurring awareness of how much Jesus has forgiven us, as we remember those who have hurt us so deeply.

● A willingness to be more vulnerable than we've ever been before.

GOD DOESN'T WASTE YOUR REGRETS

Day 1
Voice in the Darkness

Look up and read 1 Thessalonians 5.

● According to verse 4, who specifically is Paul addressing? _____

● In verses 5 and 6, note the attributes of a believer as well as those of an unbeliever.

BELIEVER	UNBELIEVER

● Turn to Ephesians 6:12 and list the four areas of struggle we encounter:

1. _____

2. _____

3. _____

4. _____

● List the four characteristics of a person encountering this struggle as noted in 1 Thessalonians 5:14:

5. _____

6. _____

7. _____

8. _____

- According to 1 Thessalonians 5:16–18:

    9. What are we to ALWAYS be doing? _____

    10. What are we to CONTINUALLY be doing? _____

    11. What is our aim for ALL circumstances? _____

- In 5:19, what specifically can be "quenched?" _____

- In 5:22, what do we "abstain" from? _____

- In 5:23, what specific things are kept blameless? _____

- According to Acts 26:15–18, what is Jesus' role as it relates to the above information?

We are all wounded people with a proclivity to hide those wounds in the dark.

Please describe one childhood wound that is still in the dark or stayed in the dark for far too long.

_____

_____

_____

What are some specific ways you kept this hurt hidden from others?

_____

_____

_____

If you've never spoken about this hurt to anyone, why not? What is the message you hear in your head when you consider opening up about the truth?

_____

_____

_____

Regret and shame always stem from unprocessed pain. The darkest parts of our story simply must surface in the light of day, or else we will only deal with that pain by causing pain to others.

Only God can heal the unresolved pain living inside us. But that healing can only begin when we decide to give _him_ complete access to the darkest parts of us.

Whose voice currently has access to the deepest part of your pain? God or the devil? (It _cannot_ be both.) To test yourself, what is the message you hear in the worst thing that's ever been done to you?

_____

What is the message you hear in the worst thing you've ever done to another?

_____

Seeing yourself in the light of day is an unnerving experience!

God doesn't wait for us to decide to listen to the right voice. He speaks straight into the darkness, our most secret places:

"Who are you listening to? Haven't I shown you how much I love you? I knew that you would doubt me before you did, and I still choose you. You are not a burden, you are my beloved."

Day 2
Peeling Back the Layers

Satan is the "ruler of darkness" for a reason. He rules the darkness because he's studied the darkness for a very long time. Satan watches and learns from our behaviors. He takes special note of the pain we've endured, and how we chose to handle that hardship. He watches for inconsistencies in our character: a weakness, temptations we easily cave to, or a specific type of personality more likely to draw out the worst in us.

Although 2 Corinthians 11:14 tells us that Satan "masquerades as an angel of light," he, along with all imposters of the faith including the hypocrite still living within each of us, will eventually be exposed by one thing . . .

Complete the verse below.

"For Satan himself masquerades as an angel of light. It is not surprising, then, if his servants also masquerade as servants of righteousness. Their end will be what their _____ **deserve." —2 Corinthians 11:14–15 (NIV)**

> (ESV) "Their end will correspond to their _____."

> (NLT) "In the end they will get the punishment their wicked _____ deserve."

> (NASB) "Therefore it is not surprising if his servants also disguise themselves as servants of righteousness, whose end will be according to their _____."

> (NKJV) "Therefore it is no great thing if his ministers also transform themselves into ministers of righteousness, whose end will be according to their _____."

None of us can help *doing* what we *believe*. That's why Jesus said, "If you love me, you will keep my commandments" (John 14:15 ESV). That's why Paul defined his mission as bringing about "the obedience of faith" among the Gentiles (Romans 1:5 ESV). It's why Hebrews 11 was written as a catalog of examples of how faith works itself out through action.

While the Bible is clear that no action or deed is right enough to save us, or wrong enough to compromise our salvation (Ephesians 2:8), our behaviors *do* help us determine the true motivation of our faith.

If we really want to know whose voice we are listening to in our deepest pain and regret, we must pay close attention to our actions, for "the mouth speaks what the heart is full of" (Matthew 12:34), and "everything we do flows from our heart" (Proverbs 4:23, paraphrase mine).

What do you know about yourself solely based on your *behaviors*? Place a checkmark next to the statement closest to being true of you in this particular category of life. (Descriptions won't be spot-on. So, go with the one that rings most true).

APPEARANCE

_____ I spend several hours a day (more than two) working on my outward appearance or researching how to make it better.

_____ On most days, I take the time (give or take an hour) to fix myself up (makeup, hair, matching clothes). I do, however, love to bum on the weekends.

_____ I don't spend much time on my outward appearance. I tend to wear the same thing every day, can't tell you the last time I washed my hair, and in general, don't care that much about "being cool or trendy."

MONEY

_____ I am extremely frugal. I don't like spending money I don't have. I enjoy budgeting, using coupons, and have little debt (if any). My friends would call me "tight."

_____ I am just as content with a table full of friends eating sandwiches at my house as I am getting dressed up to go out to a nice restaurant. I still struggle with debt and can easily justify spending money I don't have.

_____ I want all the newest gadgets and devices. Shopping, decorating, and keeping up with latest trends in home and fashion is a "rush" to my senses. I am in debt and spending money I do not have in order to maintain the lifestyle I want.

MEDIA CONSUMPTION

_____ I am rarely without my cell phone (bathroom, before bed, walking to class or my car). I scroll social media—it is a natural default for me—and I easily consume three or more hours of media each day.

_____ I definitely check social media multiple times throughout the day, but my phone is not glued to my hip. Sometimes I forget where it is.

_____ I am good with silence. I rarely check social media. My phone is mainly for texts and calls. I need daily downtime without words or noise to stay centered and at peace.

RELATIONSHIPS

_____ I am outgoing, social, and feel reenergized by spending time with people. I know a lot of people and get invited to lots of gatherings.

_____ I have a core group of friends (two or three) who know me inside and out. I tell them everything and talk to them constantly.

_____ I most often feel confident in my relationship with God, but struggle with his desire for me to be intimate and engaging in a community of people. Sometimes, I am scared to be vulnerable with the specific people God has placed in my life (spouse, coworkers, best friends, church).

SERVICE

_____ My life is busy. I work, take care of people, have a list of unmet deadlines and commitments. I say "yes" to a lot, because it makes me feel accepted and loved. I should probably say "no" more often, but it is hard for me to disappoint people.

_____ I have served charity/nonprofit groups before, but not consistently. I sign up whenever there is opportunity through my class, church, or job. Outside of my service hours, I rarely think about that particular group of people or organization.

_____ I desire to serve others every day. I want to be generous and giving with my time, but I struggle with the *sacrificial* part of service—even when serving.

Looking back at my inventory, I would say that I have learned most of my predominant behaviors from:

_____

(i.e., mom, spouse, friend, can be several people)

Satan can only speak to our *what*: the external pieces of our life—words and actions, what we say and do. But God will only and always speak to our *why*—the heart of our motive, belief, desires, and wants.

A created being himself, Satan is allowed only enough power to point out our vulnerabilities from what he observes about us. But God is the one who determines whether or not those vulnerabilities make us acceptable or unacceptable to him.

Does this inventory of your behaviors give you any new insight into *whose* voice you've been listening to?

Is there unresolved pain settled deep in your soul? Is the infection of resentment or bitterness of an unforgiven wound spreading to other areas of your life, creating harmful ways of coping? Are you attempting to deal with a serious offense in an irrational or absurd way that doesn't seem true to who you are?

Please take some time to journal below about an external behavior that is compromising your internal posture in Christ. Give specific ideas of what you are willing to do to change it? (i.e., talk about it with a trusted friend, replace it with something more productive, quit cold turkey, etc.)

_____

_____

_____

_____

Day 3
The Language of the Heart

Not only our behaviors but our *words* reveal the truest belief of our heart.

Read Luke 6:43–46 to answer the following questions:

According to the metaphor used by Jesus,

- "Fruit" represents the _____ we speak.

- From whose words do others see our reputation? (circle one):
  THEIR WORDS / MY WORDS

- Specifically, our words flow from what place? _____

- If a plant is not producing good fruit, where do we need to look to find the main problem? _____

- According to this passage, while "others" can trigger our speech, who specifically, is to "blame" for the words we speak? (circle one): **THEM / ME**

● Our words reveal the _____ desire of our heart.

Our words reveal one of two things at any given moment:

Do we trust God, or are we trying to be God?

Namely, our words reveal our true love.

If a human relationship has become our truest love, we will say most anything to keep her/him in our life. Or, if *keeping our secret* has become our greatest obsession, we will say anything in order to maintain control and justify our actions around the secret.

According to James, the way we speak is directly related to what we want. In other words, we use our words to get what is important to us.

Read James 3:1–12 to answer the following questions.

1. Although James himself is a teacher, is he fully aware of his personal shortcomings based on verse 2? _____ . Perhaps he remembers how he spoke about Jesus at the start of his ministry. What speech does James contribute to in Mark 3:21? What specifically do the disciples say about Jesus?

   _____

   _____

   _____

2. Based on James 3:3–6, list the three descriptors/specific comparisons James compares our words to:

   _____

   _____

   _____

3. Out of our mouths we are able to _____ and _____ (vs. 9). We can _____ and _____ (vs. 10).

The HORSE of COMPLAINT

Complain = {to express dissatisfaction or annoyance about a state of affairs; protesting, grumbling, whining, etc.}

Words of complaint reveal a heart hiding out in the pain of resentment. A person who is quick to see the bad in people is the person quick to see the bad in themselves.

Complaining is a common coping mechanism for the cynicism and/or bullying we may have experienced in our past.

When we are tempted to complain, we can change the way we are thinking about the troublesome issue instead. Rather than complaining about something we cannot change, we can choose to see God's love for us, even in the middle of something we would never ask for.

Placing a "bit" in the mouth of a wild horse is the only way to regain control. Without the bit, the horse is still a wild animal, capable of killing its rider. But with one small adjustment, he can be a smooth ride, capable of taking us wherever we want to go.

Can you trace a specific time of bullying, rejection, or sarcastic backlash from your past that continues to torment your present through a tendency to **complain**?

What is one small "bit" (i.e., change in perspective) you could offer to the mouth of your negative words of complaint?

The STRONG WIND of LYING

To lie = {to not tell the truth; false, two-faced, dishonest}

The devil is the father of lies. His native tongue and greatest weapon against us is *deceit*. Jesus, on the contrary, is truth. And as we know, the truth sets us free (see John 8:32).

Lies bring bondage; the truth brings freedom. Satan wants us to believe and tell a lie about who we are. He wants us to believe that our sin is just "too bad," and that the sin of others is just "too unforgiveable."

Lying is the strongest wind of sinfulness, because one "small" exaggeration or "tiny" fabrication has the ability to carry us miles away from our intended destination.

A person who feels the need to exaggerate, fabricate, or cover up the truth with their words is most likely someone struggling with unresolved shame. Shame is the fear that our honesty will be used against us. A person who uses exaggerations or distortions as self-preservation is most likely one whose been painfully mocked or rejected for their honesty in the past.

Can you describe a time in your life when shame motivated you to lie? Perhaps not a "bold-face lie," but a small distortion of the truth. How were you using this lie to cover up? What is it you do/did not want people to know?

_____

_____

_____

The SMALL SPARK of GOSSIP

Gossip = {casual or unconstrained conversation or reports about other people, typically involving details that are not confirmed as being true}

> **"When arguing with your neighbor, don't betray another person's secret. Others may accuse you of gossip, and you will never regain your good reputation."**
> **Proverbs 25:9–10 NLT**

> **"If another believer sins against you, go privately and point out the offense. If the other person listens and confesses it, you have won that person back."**
> **Matthew 18:15 NLT**

"Hey, did you hear . . . ?" is the only lead one typically needs for words to become a morsel that sinks deep into our heart (see Proverbs 18:8). We love gossip because it's tasty and sweet. Such words give us a bit of an advantage, edge, or put us "in the know"—like chewing on a rich, delicious piece of candy. As long as we are in control of the calorie intake, gossip tastes good. But the moment we are on the receiving end of being gossiped about, nausea sets in.

The truth is, everything that is said should be true. But not everything that is true should be said.

Knowing the truth about someone does not give us permission to repeat it.

When someone begins to share details with us about another person, we can simply respond with, "Hey, have you had a chance to talk to _____ about this?" Or, "Let's wait for _____ to get here to talk about this."

As Jesus teaches in Matthew 18, if we have something against a person or if we simply need to talk though something for clarity, we are to go directly to the person and have a one-on-one conversation. In love, we are to protect the privacy of others, working overtime to keep our words few and as intimate as possible.

Gossip reveals the part of our past we still seek to control. One who gossips is most likely one who has not yet taken the time to think and talk through the most embarrassing, painful parts of their story. Therefore, they use their words to control the amount of information others know about them.

Think about the last time you initiated a conversation that would be considered "gossip." How might you have been deflecting unwanted attention from yourself onto another? What specifically could you have been trying to hide in doing so?

_____

_____

Our words are one of the ways we gain, maintain, and keep what is most important to us.

If hiding our most painful, embarrassing parts has become our first love, we will battle anyone who attempts to uncover those stories. But if our greatest love is God, if we need _his_ love more than anyone else, our words will reflect the heart of a woman secure and confident in the love of her life.

When Jesus is our greatest love, the outflow of both our words and actions will be the life-giving nourishment of fresh, sweet fruit.

To end our day, please write out the fruit of the Spirit listed for us in Galatians 5:22–23. You should have nine total:

_____ _____ _____

_____ _____ _____

_____ _____ _____

Day 4
Feeding Stray Lions

Growing up, my grandmother would say, "If you want to keep a stray dog away, stop feeding him."

She was rightly teaching me how to deal with sinful patterns of behavior in my life.

As a child, things like not sharing and fighting with my brother were easier to stop feeding. But as I got older, my secret life of sexual promiscuity, self-sabotage, and manipulation felt less like a stray dog scratching at the door for scraps and more like, well, this . . .

Be *sober-minded*; be watchful.
Your adversary the devil prowls around like a *roaring* lion,
seeking someone to devour.
1 Peter 5:8 ESV, emphasis mine

According to 2 Timothy 2:24–26, *who* is the person snared by the devil and captured to do his will.

_____ **an atheist**   _____ **the servant of the Lord**   _____ **a rebel without cause**

According to Psalm 19:13, who is capable of willful (on purpose) sin?

_____ **a servant of the Lord**   _____ **a drug dealer**   _____ **a soccer mom**

According to Galatians 6:1, what type of person can be caught in sin and/or tempted to sin?

_____ **people who don't go to church**   _____ **people who go to church**

According to 2 Corinthians 11:3, what type of devotion can be led away from Jesus?

_____ and _____

First Corinthians 10:6 tells us that the Old Testament was given that we might not desire what?

_____

Galatians 5:16–26 tells us that when we know we BELONG to Jesus, we will be able to "crucify _____"

and "keep in step with the _____."

If we are struggling with overt, obvious behaviors that are painful to us and bringing harm to others, we need to stop.

Or as Jesus puts it, "If your hand causes you to sin, cut it off." (Matthew 5:30 ESV)

Jesus does not mince words here.

Throughout the Bible, God plainly teaches us the first, most practical step to put an end to behaviors that hold us captive in a habitual way—do whatever it takes to stop doing them. (Or in the words of my Gran, "stop feeding the stray dog.")

Habitual Sin = {a pattern of behavior that enjoys the experience of the behavior more than the experience of God}

Satan has a doctorate in human behavior. While he's studied us for a very long time, he cannot read the future any more than we can. He is left only to tempt us to distrust God based on what he sees us *do*.

> "Come now, let us reason together, says the LORD:
> though your sins are like scarlet,
> they shall be as white as snow;
> though they are red like crimson,
> they shall become like wool."
>
> **Isaiah 1:18**

Based on this verse from Isaiah, what is the act that precedes the full cleansing of our sin? _____

Once we give voice to a specific internal battle, you can bet that Satan and his demons are on the ready to use that confession against us. But here's the good news—the moment we expose our pain, we have also exposed the enemy's *only* weapon of attack. Our confession greatly weakens his plan to destroy us.

Regret turns to captivity when we are unwilling to "reason" about our past. It makes sense that Satan would use all his resources to keep us alone and isolated in our sin, repeating the lie that we are not worth anyone's time and energy, namely God's.

Write down one area of your life you are willing to "bring to the light" this week. It may be an area of ongoing habitual sin that is destroying your mind and relationships, or it may be a place of pain that will become habitual if you don't give voice to it soon.

Isaiah 43:25 says that God *"remembers your sins no more."* But God forgetting and humans forgetting are two very different things. God, of course, remembers everything, but through Christ's sacrifice, holds nothing against us—neither the sinful choices we have yet to confess nor the ones we have yet to commit.

There is a great *misconception* floating around out there that true healing only comes once we no longer feel connected to the sinful thoughts and behaviors of our past. This instruction is unbiblical and dangerously reinforces the harmful behavior we are attempting to kick.

Attempting to forget the great lengths which Christ has gone to save us slows the healing process and alienates us from real life with real people.

Read Ephesians 2:1–10, then answer the following:

1. According to verse 3, WHO once lived according to their flesh?

2. In verse 5, WHEN are we healed (made alive in Christ)?

3. According to verse 10, WHAT was prepared beforehand?

We will never be free of "big" or "little" habits until we level the playing field between "big" and "little."

This is the primary message Jesus brings with his kingdom—the *why*, not the what. Worry and adultery carry very different external consequences, but they are equally lethal to our hearts.

When you consider your ability to sin and simultaneously feel intense panic, shame, or pride rise to the surface, this can be a clear indicator of a place from your past that is beckoning your remembrance. However, if your own capacity to do "the worst of the worst" slams into a wall of humility, gratitude, or sorrow, you are remembering from the right place.

Condemnation = {lingering shame leading to pride}

Conviction = {short-term guilt leading to sorrow}

Based on 1 John 3:19–21, how do we know we are remembering our past from the right place—living in confidence, not condemnation?

There is no part of our past or present that God is not weaving into the good and beautiful tapestry of his eternal purposes. In light of this truth, we must fight the whisper of the enemy telling us, "It's all over," "You're done," or "You've blown it too bad."

Are there things you are concealing in the darkness, afraid to expose to the light? Do not be afraid. Instead, let Jesus's perfect love for you cast out your fear (1 John 4:18). His word to you is this: "I have come into the world as light, so that whoever believes in me may not remain in darkness" (John 12:46 ESV). Jesus offers you complete forgiveness and cleansing (see 1 John 1:9) and eternal life (see John 3:16).

Come to the Light and really live.

Day 5
Godly Regret

"For godly grief produces a repentance that leads to salvation without regret, whereas worldly grief produces death."
2 Corinthians 7:10 ESV

1. According to this verse, is there a type of grief over our regret that is good? **YES / NO**

2. What specifically does "godly grief" produce? _____

3. What specifically does "worldly grief" produce? _____

4. Using the definition below, how has God used a past grief to bring you to repentance?

Repentance = {a decision to start trusting God in an area where you once distrusted him}

_____

_____

5. Give an example of how someone might display "worldly grief" over their sin:

_____

_____

6. According to Matthew 27:3–5, how did "worldly grief" effect Judas?

_____

7. According to Matthew 26:75 how did "godly grief" effect Peter?

_____

Both Peter and Judas stood in the presence of Jesus. And each chose to betray him.

While both Peter _and_ Judas experienced true grief over their choice to distrust God, only one of them used the pain of that regret to recommit his life to Christ. Peter believed the truth. The forgiveness of Jesus went further than his choice to sin against him. But Judas believed the lie that he was too far gone to receive the forgiveness of Christ.

What about you? Who do you relate to more, Peter or Judas? When you think back on the ways you've distrusted or blatantly rebelled against God, do you believe his forgiveness is enough?

_____

_____

_____

It's one thing to tell others about the love and forgiveness of Christ. But quite another to receive his love and forgiveness for ourselves.

Take a moment to read Psalm 107 carefully. In the space provided below each passage, describe how your personal life of sin and sorrow has ebbed and flowed as described by the psalmists.

Verses 5–6

_____

_____

_____

When have you felt like a wanderer because of your sin, unsettled by your regret? Describe how you cried out and the way God delivered you.

_____

_____

_____

Verses 10–14

_____

_____

_____

Describe a time in your life when God used the consequence of a sinful decision as the very thing that exposed the darkness and brought you to the light of truth.

_____

_____

Verses 17–20

_____

_____

Was there a season of life when rebellious choices felt so good that they made you stupid for more—but in the end they made you sick? If applicable, describe how God's Word healed you during this time?

_____

_____

_____

Verses 23–29

_____

_____

_____

Is there a time in your life when you regret letting your religious zeal get the best of you? A time when you thought you were better than others because of your relationship with God? Describe how you cried out to God during this time, and how he calmed the waves of approval.

_____

_____

_____

The truth is, no matter how dark it's gotten, how lost you've felt, God has never left your side! Even on your worst days, he has been right there—loving you, pleading with you, blessing you. His love for you is unchanging and steady, not dampened by how many drags you take or days of prayer you forsake.

Hoping in Jesus does not mean we will be released from pain, reconciled to all relationships, or receive the answers to our burning questions. But it _does_ mean we have everything we need, right this very moment, to grieve our greatest regrets, choose truth, receive healing from God, and enjoy the life he's given us—wounds and all.

Read the conclusion of Psalm 107—verses 30–36—and note below the parts that comfort you most right now.

_____

_____

_____

SESSION 4

GOD DOESN'T WASTE YOUR PAIN

This is a great week to read chapters 11–13 in the book!

Introduction (5 MINUTES)

Leader, please read aloud to group:

One of the most breathtaking facts about God is that he doesn't just ask us to trust him; he also plans out moments to show himself faithful beyond our wildest imaginations. Sometimes God allows our situations to go from bad to worse. Sometimes we'll even get to the point that we say, "God, I can't do this anymore." And it's often in those precise moments that he delights in blowing us away with something bigger and better than if he'd intervened the way we asked him to.

How would it change your perspective on your struggles if you realized that every difficult circumstance you endure can be a setup for God's greatness and faithfulness to be displayed in your life?

God sets us up to experience him in fresh, new ways in and through our waiting and our trials. The question is, how will we respond to the setup in our most painful season of life?

Will we throw away our faith and try to take matters into our own hands? Or will we keep trusting, even when we can't see the big picture? *"Do not throw away this confident trust in the Lord. Remember the great reward it brings you!"* (Hebrews 10:35 NLT)

When God allows pain in our life, he is preparing for us something greater than we could ever arrange, manipulate, or think up. As we faithfully trust him *through* the hardship, we will begin to understand a revolutionary truth—God's purpose for our lives will never be found in the result, only through the process.

In fact, his process *is* the point!

"I waited patiently for the LORD;
he turned to me and heard my cry.
He lifted me out of the slimy pit,
out of the mud and mire;
he set my feet on a rock
and gave me a firm place to stand.
He put a new song in my mouth,
a hymn of praise to our God.
Many will see and fear the LORD
and put their trust in him."

Psalm 40:1–3

Video Session Four (21 MINUTES)

Watch Video Session 4 and fill in the blanks below.

1. Sometimes the love of Jesus _____ .

2. The most unexplainable and awful hardship is fixed to _____ _____ where we stand with Jesus.

3. God will never linger out of wrath or anger, but out of pure and holy desire for us to trust him more _____ than we did _____ .

"Father, if you are willing, take this cup from
me; yet not my will, but yours be done."

Luke 22:42

4. It is only good and right for God to remind us: His _____ is at _____ no matter how much we _____ .

5. His _____ is the _____.

6. Satan is only allowed to mess with us to the degree our sin is sifted and _____ in our life.

7. To the degree we doubt our _____ is the degree we disbelieve God's _____.

8. Without laying claim to the gift rightfully ours in God, we will never be fully _____.

> "And since we have a great priest over the house of
> God, let us draw near to God with a sincere heart
> and with the full assurance that faith brings."
> **Hebrews 10:21–22**

> "And I pray that you, being rooted and established in love, may
> have power, together with all the Lord's holy people, to grasp
> how wide and long and high and deep is the love of Christ,
> and to know this love that surpasses knowledge—that you
> may be filled to the measure of all the fullness of God."
> **Ephesians 3:18–19**

YOU KNOW THAT'S RIGHT.

Use this space to take notes of your own:

_____

_____

_____

_____

Group Discussion Questions (30 MINUTES)

1. Pain left unchecked is a dangerous force to our mind, body, and soul. The pain itself is not the danger; rather, it's the message in the pain. What are some examples of dangerous messages we receive in the midst of our pain? (i.e., loss, rejection, abuse, misunderstanding, divorce, hurting children, financial crisis, etc.)

2. Why does Satan choose to speak often and loud to us in the midst of our pain? What might be the mission of his message?

3. God also speaks to us in pain. What is the mission of his message?

4. Allow a few people to share the most significant experience of suffering they have gone through. What happened and how did it affect them?

5. Share a time in your life when God used pain and tragedy to bring you closer to him. How did you respond?

SESSION 4 FOCUS:

God does not waste our pain.

He uses suffering and tragedy in life to increase our faith and reveal our purpose.

Closing Prayer

(lead out or ask a volunteer)

Points of prayer for Session Four:

- Unity with others in the fact that no one gets through life unscathed by tragedy and hardship.

- Openness to a new perspective regarding our most painful experiences.

- Peace of mind that not all our painful experiences are meant to be understood.

- Willingness to acknowledge that while the painful experience may not have been sinful, we may need to confess the sinful ways we responded to the crisis.

- Sense of excitement over the way God wants to reveal his purpose and meaning for our lives through our pain, not in spite of it.

PERSONAL BIBLE STUDY Session 4

GOD DOESN'T WASTE YOUR PAIN

Day 1
Another Side to Suffering

We've been taught that God is love and that he is a good Father—and he absolutely is. But Scripture makes it clear that God is also willing to use drastic measures to get our attention. In fact, some of God's greatest acts of love for us come through pain. Like a parent taking the training wheels off a child's bike or letting him fight his own battles, God knows that sometimes the most loving thing he can do is to let us fall down, get hurt, and live to fight another day.

Look up and read the following passages.

Below each passage, in your own words, describe how you see God relating to man. (Think: What part of God's nature is mankind being asked to experience?)

Job 3:20–26

Psalm 13:1–2

Matthew 16:24–25

2 Corinthians 1:8–9

James 1:2–4

These passages barely skim the surface of believers who experience painful suffering by the governing authority of God. In fact, if Scripture is any indication, suffering isn't the exception for believers; it seems to be the default. There's a long line of faithful followers of Christ who have gone before us and have the black eyes, broken bones, and bloody noses to show for it.

Describe a time you felt as though God allowed a painful experience to play out in your life. What happened? How did you respond to God in that moment?

Suffering can come in many forms. It may come as a result of another person's sin or simply from living in a fallen world. We may suffer from grief, from a broken relationship with a loved one, from sickness, from financial strain, or from persecution that comes as a result of following Christ. When the things that give us security and enjoyment— money, reputation, health, children, self-esteem, relationships, success—are taken away, either by force or by choice, we suffer. Whatever the specific circumstances, we often find our faith shaken, and we ask, "How could you, God?"

Journal about a personal time of suffering that caused you to wonder, "Why, God?" Do you still question him about this? If so, what are your questions for him?

_____

_____

_____

Suffering has a way of bringing us into the depths of knowing Jesus in a way we can never experience when our lives are "comfortable" and "happy." Suffering is an essential part of the created universe in which the greatness of God's grace can be most fully known.

Everything that Christ accomplished for us, he accomplished by suffering.

Everything that we will ever truly enjoy in life will come to us because of suffering.

> **"But he was pierced for our transgressions,**
> **he was crushed for our iniquities;**
> **the punishment that brought us peace was on him,**
> **and by his wounds we are healed."**
> **Isaiah 53:5**

Day 2
Lingering Love

> **"Remember the things I have done in the past. For I alone am God! I am God, and there is none like me. Only I can tell you the future before it even happens. Everything I plan will come to pass, for I do whatever I wish."**
> **Isaiah 46:9–10 NLT**

The sovereignty of God is one of those big, hairy pieces of biblical doctrine, leaving no human unchanged who dares approach the reality of it.

We may claim to believe that God is sovereign, but that conviction is tested when tragedy strikes. When we're holding the hand of someone who has just lost her child or spouse or parent and her weeping eyes look into ours, how do we respond? When a terrorist detonates a bomb that kills hundreds of civilians or a tornado rips through a nearby town or children go hungry, what do we believe to be true of God? The words that come out of our mouths often stand contrary to the truth that God is, in fact, governing even the most terrible tragedies.

Perhaps the reality is, we don't know what to say.

Read John 11:1–44.

Based on verse 3, how would you describe Lazarus's relationship with Jesus?

It seems only right for Jesus to stop what he's doing and hightail it to Lazarus's house upon hearing of his friend's terminal illness. I mean, he was only one day's travel away. And yet . . .

Based on verse 6, how many days did Jesus wait before he left for Bethany? _____

The Bible makes it clear there was a strong friendship between Jesus and Lazarus, yet Jesus' actions seem to contradict this truth. And perhaps even more hard-hitting is the fact that Jesus, being God in flesh, already knew that Lazarus was sick before the messenger told him. He knew Lazarus would die from the sickness before he would make it there. In short, Jesus loved Lazarus and still let him die.

Think of a time in your life when your circumstance seemed to contradict a God of love. A time of suffering when you expected Jesus to rescue you, but he didn't. Journal the emotions you felt at that time.

_____

_____

What request have you brought before God that he has yet to answer?

_____

_____

Fill in the blanks in verses 5–6:

"Now Jesus _____ Martha and her sister and Lazarus. _____ when he heard that Lazarus was sick, he _____ was two more days."

So—a small but important word to help us understand how God's nature perfectly aligns with his predetermined will in all things. From the outflow of God's love, he waited two more days.

He could have gone to Bethany earlier, healed Lazarus before he died, and had a party to celebrate afterward. But instead, the love of Jesus lingered. The motivation for letting Lazarus suffer and die? Love.

The disciples responded to Jesus' methods about the same way we mortals respond to the topic of God's sovereignty. "Huh?" "What?" "But that doesn't make sense." "Let's do this instead."

Based on verses 11–13, what big lesson did the disciples totally miss?

_____

_____

Jesus knew he would wait two days until Lazarus was not just a little bit dead, but a lot dead. Jesus chose his actions wisely, for they would impact many people—the disciples, Martha and Mary, the extended family grieving alongside them, and the whole community. It was not Jesus who needed a lesson in faith. Jesus didn't need to know where these people stood in their faith—*they* needed to know for themselves why they believed what they believed. Everyone within the impact zone of this tragedy was about to get a serious lesson in believing God despite their circumstance.

According to Jesus' words in verse 15, what spiritual blessing will the disciples receive because Jesus chose to linger in love? _____

Based on your specific track record, what is characteristically common of you when hard times hit and the love of God seems to linger far too long? Place a check mark next to the activities and/or emotions you tend to engage during times of suffering, crisis, and/or tragedy.

_____ I have the desire to pick up an old vice, such as _____
(i.e., drinking, smoking, binge watching TV, ODing on diet soda, eating junk food, shopping, etc.)

_____ I throw myself into work or extra projects. I'd rather distract myself with business than deal with my feelings around pain.

_____ I retreat from anything/anyone that would trigger my emotions. I stay away from intimate conversations with friends, even withhold affection from my children, spouse, and family, in attempts not to cry or get angry about the pain I'm experiencing.

_____ I go to church less often, because the idea that God is allowing this is too painful.

_____ I go to church more often, because I am desperate for answers.

_____ My closest friends could not tell you the details of what I am going through.

_____ My closest friends are my lifeline in suffering; I tell them everything.

_____ Crisis causes me to feel overwhelmed. I have trouble sleeping, feel anxious, and the thoughts of my situation consume me.

_____ Crisis causes me to feel really ticked off. I start to snap at people, act irrationally, and consider ways I might rebel against God because he let this happen.

_____ I pray more.

_____ I pray less.

_____ I read my Bible more.

_____ I read my Bible less.

Suffering tends to trigger a cascade of bad reactions. God gives a cascade of better reasons that invite the finest responses of which a human being is capable.

Read Isaiah 40:27–31 and make note of God's promises to us in the midst of suffering:

_____

_____

_____

_____

Day 3
Great Awakening

Let's continue with Lazarus's story through the eyes of Martha.

Read John 11:17–23 (NLT).

As Martha wept, I picture Jesus gently lifting her face to meet his and then, with loving intensity, speaking over her, "Your brother will rise again."

"He will rise when everyone else rises, at the last day," she finally said (vs. 24). Martha most likely had no idea Jesus was referring to something more in that moment.

He replied, **"I am the resurrection and the life. Anyone who believes in me will live, even after dying. Everyone who lives in me and believes in me will never ever die. Do you believe this?" (verses 25–26).**

The power of Jesus' words must have caused faith to swell in Martha's soul—an awakening, one might say. I doubt she was sure what it all meant, but as Jesus spoke, it was as if death itself was being swallowed up (see 1 Corinthians 15:54). No one else had ever spoken like this man (see John 7:46).

Martha answered, **"I have always believed you are the Messiah, the Son of God, the one who has come into the world from God" (vs. 27).**

Has there ever been a time when your soul was on fire for the truth of God despite the pain around you? Describe that experience below.

Check the TRUE statements based on 2 Corinthians 4:7–18.

_____ The strength given us to endure hardship is compared to that of a "treasure."

_____ We are hard pressed on a few sides, but not all sides.

_____ It's okay to be confused in the midst of pain.

_____ A lot of bad things may happen, but persecution's not one of them.

_____ We really are alone in tragedy.

_____ Only when things get really bad do we identify with the death of Jesus.

_____ The very life of Jesus is revealed in us through our suffering.

_____ The benefit of all this pain we are enduring is that more and more people might understand God's grace.

_____ It is possible not to lose heart!

_____ Our outward appearance is not at all compromised by pain.

_____ Our troubles are heavy and long-lasting.

_____ Our faith gives us eyes to see what is really going on in suffering.

Before we know what Jesus is doing, circumstances can look all wrong, and we're tempted to interpret God's apparent inaction as a lack of love. But in fact, God is showing us love in the most profound way. The question for us is the same as it was for Martha when Jesus peered into her eyes and asked, "Do you believe this?"

List some areas in your life where you are currently aware that God is doing something greater than you can see here and now.

_____

_____

_____

Nothing in this universe exists for its own sake.

Everything, from the sunrise each morning to the final breath of our loved ones, exists to make Christ's glory more fully known.

I don't know about you, but I don't want to serve a God who simply sits by and allows things to happen on this earth. I desire to worship an all-knowing, all-powerful, all-sovereign God who controls everything. Even the things I don't understand.

Day 4
Storms of Faith

Read Matthew 14:13–21 and Matthew 14:22–36.

Note the contrast between victory and storm of these back-to-back stories in Scripture.

Our "trials by storm" often hit us directly after great moments of victory or celebration. Can you think of a time this has been true for you? Describe the victory you experienced and then describe the storm that came soon after.

Victory: _____

Storm: _____

_____

Victory: _____

Storm: _____

_____

Victory: _____

Storm: _____

Write the first half of Matthew 14:26 here:

_____

What did Peter do in Matthew 14:28–29?

_____

_____

In your own words, describe why you think Peter began to sink? What was he thinking/feeling in that moment?

_____

_____

Interestingly, the Bible never tells us that Peter *took his eyes off Jesus*. The text says instead, "he *saw* the wind."

Poor guy gets a bad rap in most sermon messages for "taking his eyes off Jesus," but maybe he didn't. Maybe, like so many of us in our storms of suffering, we are staring straight in to the eyes of Jesus when tragedy strikes.

Perhaps, like Peter, the pain of life does not crush our faith completely. Just decreases it substantially.

> **"But when he saw the wind, he was afraid and,**
> **beginning to sink, cried out, 'Lord, save me!'**
> **Immediately Jesus reached out his hand and caught him.**
> **'You of little faith,' he said, 'why did you doubt?'"**
> **Matthew 14:30–31**

Place a check mark next to the distractions that tend to create the most chaos in the periphery of your faith. Not causing you to doubt God completely but tempting you to consider it. (Check all that apply.)

_____ my busy schedule

_____ the needs of other people

_____ the demands of my job

_____ social commitments

_____ phone, email, internet, social media

_____ a dysfunctional or strained relationship

_____ my marriage

_____ my rebellious child

_____ my anger toward someone

_____ my bitterness toward someone

Sometimes our greatest storms, trials, fears, and doubts come when we're looking smack-dab into the face of Jesus.

I don't see Peter as someone who lacked faith. Instead, I see him as man of faith, who God set up to receive even more.

Remember, Peter is the only one who got out of the boat.

Peter asked Jesus to tell him to come. Jesus honored Peter's faith by commanding the water to bear his weight, teaching Peter a significant lesson:

Real faith doesn't come from *our* ability to be faithful but from *God's* ability to be faithful.

Jesus was capable of holding Peter up that day, but had Jesus never let him sink just a little, Peter would never have experienced a deeper, more intimate dependence on the Lord.

The grace of God allowed Peter to sink slowly, instead of sinking quickly like a stone in water. And the love of God allowed Peter to know that whatever storms he would face in the future, God would always be there—reaching out his hand to catch us.

Describe a time when God allowed you to "sink" just long enough for you to cry out in dependence upon him. In what ways did you experience God's love and grace through that process?

After his faith lesson on the water, Peter had highs and lows in his life. Peter would "see the wind" throughout the remainder of his life. He would be tempted over and over to distrust God in the midst of life's most dangerous storms.

Yet every time, despite Peter's faithlessness, God was faithful.

Oh how I *pray* the hardships of life send us all into a unified echo of this motley crew of fishermen, collecting their wits and cheering through laughter and tears.

> **"Then those who were in the boat worshiped him, saying, 'Truly you are the Son of God.'"**
> **Matthew 14:33**

Day 5
Outside the Camp

What part of this study thus far is compelling to you dig deeper in your relationship with Christ?

_____

_____

Read 1 Peter 4:12–19.

What are three truths we learn about suffering from this passage?

1. _____

2. _____

3. _____

Faith anchors everything we do and everything we are as followers of Christ. It's the only way we can have a close, intimate relationship with him.

I want you to know a faith that wrestles with hard questions and takes God up on liberating truths like:

- What God permits, he permits for a reason. (Job 42:11)

- Suffering is a gift, not a curse. (Psalm 84:11)

- Pain is God's way of offering us complete dependence on him. (2 Corinthians 1:9)

- Crisis is meant to draw us deeper into relationships, not solitude. (Philippians 2:26–27)

- Tragedy is our way to be done with sin, finally and fully. (Luke 9:25)

In order to embrace a deeper level of faith, we need to understand what Scripture says is true about faith.

Draw a line matching the verse on the left to its corresponding truth on the right.

Romans 10:17	Faith is powerful enough to fight evil.
Galatians 5:6	We will only understand faith through hearing God's word.
Hebrews 11:6	We are made right in God's sight through faith.
Ephesians 6:16	Faith isn't about ceremony or ritual; it's expressed through love.
Romans 1:17	Without faith we cannot please God.

Read Hebrews 13:12–14.

This passage says that Jesus goes "outside the camp "or "outside the gates."

What do you think that means?

_____

The writer of Hebrews was most likely referencing the Israelites' mobile community that would settle for a time along a river or in a mountain valley. A camp was a place of safety for people. If you went outside the camp, you'd face dangers including wild animals, enemies, and the obvious threat of being vulnerable to the elements. The camp was a place of comfort, safety, and familiarity. In addition, according to Jewish tradition, the camp represented all that was sacred in their society, while everything outside the camp was considered unclean.

So, when the author tells us to join Jesus "outside the camp," it's as if he is saying, "Hey, you—take a risk with me, be dangerous, step out of your comfort zone, be willing to get a little dirty."

When we step outside our "camp" of religious safety, we encounter people who don't look like us, talk like us, or act like us. Some places outside the camp are uncomfortable, muddy, and downright scary. But there are lost and needy men, women, and children who are living in darkness and in need of the light we can bring from the warm, safe huddle of our camp.

Who in your life is "outside the camp"? What would it look like to bring light to them?

_____

_____

_____

Write about a time you took a risk for God. What was the experience like? How did you feel before you went for it? How did you feel when it was all over?

Write about a time you felt God asking you to take a risk and you chose not to do it. What regrets did you have afterward?

What holds you back from taking risks for God?

Do you want this life-changing, gut-wrenching, as-close-as-your-breath faith? If so, you have to be willing to go outside the camp.

Read Philippians 1:29.

This passage makes the surprising statement that it's not only a privilege to trust Christ but also a privilege to do what? How might this change your perspective on suffering?

Read Hebrews 2:18.

What does it mean to you that Jesus went through suffering and testing himself?

_____

_____

Read James 5:11.

What does the story of Job show us about God's character and how he treats us in the long term?

_____

_____

May we be willing to empty everything before him—our illnesses, our betrayals, our unforgiving hearts, our addictions, our depression, our insecurity, our pride, our money, our complacency, our damage, our stupidity, our brokenness, our small-mindedness. As we ponder faith in its purest, most organic, whole form, may his Word come alive before our eyes.

In the darkest night of pain, trial, and suffering, may this truth resound in the recesses of our hearts:

> "The LORD is the everlasting God, the Creator of all the earth.
> He never grows weak or weary. No one can measure the depths of his
> understanding. He gives power to the weak and strength to the powerless.
> Even youths will become weak and tired, and young men will fall in
> exhaustion. But those who trust in the LORD will find new strength.
> They will soar high on wings like eagles. They will run and not grow weary.
> They will walk and not faint."
> **Isaiah 40:28–31 NLT**

SESSION 5

GOD DOESN'T WASTE YOUR NATURE

This is a great week to read chapters 14–16 in the book!

Introduction (5 MINUTES)

Leader, please read aloud to group:

> **"When I consider your heavens, the work of your fingers,**
> **the moon and the stars, which you have set in place,**
> **what is mankind that you are mindful of them,**
> **human beings that you care for them?**
> **You have made them a little lower than the angels**
> **and crowned them with glory and honor."**
>
> **Psalm 8:3–5**

There is nothing more popular in our modern-day culture than the search for *meaning*. We see the wide range of theories on how to answer this question glaring at us on store bookshelves. We hear our options streamed constantly over social media and through inspirational messages. Personality tests, like the *Myers-Briggs* and the *Enneagram*, have received growing attention over the past decade in particular, due to humans becoming ever-increasingly aware of their need for truth.

Despite self-help as a now spoon-fed delicacy, we continue to obsess over the same questions year after year—"Who am I?" "What am I here for?" "How can I find myself!"

The truth is, we all desperately want to know that *who we are* is valued and desired.

We all want to be loved.

And if we're honest, there is a small part in each one of us that truly believes no one will want or love us just the way we are. We continue to wrestle with the aggravating possibility that something inside us is broken. That if we can't "fix" this broken part in us, rejection is imminent.

Doesn't it make sense, then, that an entire generation of humans are chanting, "Be you!" "Do you!" "You are who you say you are!" "You can be whoever you want to be!"

As long as we "are who we say we are," we can isolate ourselves from intimate relationships in order to protect ourselves from the pain of rejection. If my "best self" is inside me, then no one outside me can expect or require change. If a personality test or self-help book can quickly point me to a "category" of "like" people, then, my unique nuances, no matter how destructive, are a bit more justifiable.

The Bible, however, gives us a completely different alternative to modern-day self-meaning. Psalm 8 (page 118) is a prime example that our real self, our truest self, can only be found by beholding and basking in the glory and honor of a holy God. That every part of our past, and how it's shaped our present demeanor, is "cared for" and crafted by a Creator who thinks about us, designs us, and places within each one of us a unique personality and calling through which to know him more.

The more we see the greatness of God, the more we see the greatness of ourselves and others. On the other hand, the less we acknowledge the glory of God, the less we will honor the diversity and complexity of being human.

Video Session Five (19 MINUTES)

Watch Video Session 5 and fill in the blanks below.

1. He _____ his nature into us.

2. One problem keeping us stuck in old ways: _____.

3. It is hard to _____ what we don't _____.

4. First, we can be ignorant of _____.

> **"Resist him, firm in your faith, knowing that the same kinds of suffering are being experienced by your brotherhood throughout the world."**
>
> **1 Peter 5:9 ESV**

5. Despite our differences, one thing connects us: _____.

6. Second, we can be ignorant of our own _____.

7. God wants to show us _____, so that we will know fully _____.

8. Fill in blanks below.

    We can act outside of our knowledge, but we can never act outside our (1) _____.

    Just because a way seems right doesn't mean it is (2) _____.

    People cannot make us do anything, but they can (3) _____.

    (4) _____ is not the truth-teller.

9. When we delight in God, our nature can roam freely as our _____, not our _____.

10. Our _____ is God's raw material for the new thing he is building.

COME ON WITH IT!

Use this space to take notes of your own:

_____

_____

_____

Group Discussion Questions (30 MINUTES)

1. How would you describe your personality? Example: Are you an introvert/extrovert? Controlling or go with the flow? Avoid conflict or welcome it? Please take a few minutes to share your perceived personality attributes with the group.

2. How big of a role did your parents (the people who raised you) play in shaping your personality? When was the last time you thought, "That sounded like my mother," or "I did that just like my father"?

3. What part of you do you feel was given to honor God and serve others? In other words, have you discovered your personal gift and/or calling in life? If yes, how do you use it for the Lord? If no, why not?

4. What is your big, hairy dream? If money was no object and fear was out of the question, what would you do with the rest of your life?

5. How do you receive rebuke or opinion about the parts of you that may need to change? What parts of your personality do you feel are set in stone (if any), and what parts of you still need tempering? Please explain how you know this.

SESSION 5 FOCUS:

God does not waste our personality.

He uses the shape of our life to lead us to the unique gift and calling he's chosen to bring glory to himself and honor to others.

Closing Prayer

(lead out or ask a volunteer)

Points of prayer for Session Five:

- An open mind to the fact that our "ideal" self and "true" self may be two different people.

- Courage to believe we are uniquely designed to receive spiritual, supernatural gifts.

- Desperation that God's glory be known above our own.

- Tender, soft heart toward the parts of us in need of correction and tempering.

- A desire to change the parts of our personalities that are not loving other people well.

PERSONAL BIBLE STUDY Session 5

GOD DOESN'T WASTE YOUR PERSONALITY

Day 1
Storyology

My son's baseball coach is a legitimate, professional gold prospector. For the past twenty years, he's traveled to Alaska, where he spends weeks ankle deep in a mountain stream panning for gold. I've stayed late after practice on numerous occasions, fascinated by his stories of expedition. This week of study, in particular, brings me back to warm, spring evenings sitting with him in the dugout as he replays his obsession.

Our life, like gold mining, is full of big, obvious moments. If our life were like coach's pan, we'd have no problem filling it with the sands of time. Large, rock-size materials like our relationships, regrets, and pain, glare at us from below the surface of the water; the mud and silt of our life choices often floating to the top first.

All of the materials matter to the integrity of the expedition, but the most treasured parts of our lives must be slowly and carefully sifted out. Forward and back, gently then vigorously, until all that's left in our pan are tiny specks of shimmering flakes. Often times, barely noticeable to the untrained eye.

First Peter 1:6–7 compares the genuineness of our faith to what? _____

Based on these verses, gold becomes more valuable through what process?

_____

What is the intended result of trial by fire?

_____

_____

If gemology is the science and study of precious jewels, then I say, this week is our chance for "storyology"—the science and study of the value of our life story.

Do you think the story of your life is worth thinking about? Explain the possible benefits of examining the people and experiences that have shaped you.

How do you think our post-modern culture has missed the mark when it comes to self-evaluation and awareness? Can we be overly consumed with self-perception? If so, how?

How do the following verses encourage us to take time for self-awareness? Next to each passage, write the specific thing God is commanding us to consider and/or remember (use modern day language to explain):

Deuteronomy 8:18

Deuteronomy 9:7

Deuteronomy 32:7

Psalm 42:4

Ecclesiastes 11:8

Matthew 5:23–24 _____

Hebrews 10:32 _____

Hebrews 13:7 _____

Revelation 3:3 _____

It's easy to get caught up in the "catching up."

God's Word is saturated with his petition for us to slow down, think about, and study the shape of our lives, specifically, how *he* has written a unique story in to each one of us.

Before heading in to our next day of study, please take a moment to dig around in the stream of your thoughts.

Checkmark the box under each personality characteristic that most accurately describes you present-day:

SOCIAL

_____ I am rejuvenated being around people.

_____ I am exhausted being around people.

_____ I enjoy social interaction, but require solitude for recharge.

I know I've reached my social engagement limit when I _____.

FACIAL EXPRESSION

_____ People often know exactly how I feel based on my facial expressions.

_____ People have a hard time reading me. I'm not often expressive with my face.

_____ I like to keep people guessing, so, I monitor my expressions closely.

EMOTION

_____ I have big feelings. It's easy for me to cry, easy for me to laugh. I like to feel!

_____ I have big feelings but, it's unlikely I trust you enough to show you.

_____ Feelings make me feel weak and out of control. I'd rather rationalize my way to the next thought or idea.

RELATIONAL

_____ My pattern in relationships is two or three "ride or die" friends, with everyone else as good acquaintances.

_____ I've never had a "best friend" per say. Just a bunch of really good friends.

_____ I keep pretty much everyone at arm's length. I can't think of one person who really knows the depths of me.

CONFLICT

_____ I avoid conflict like the plague. I'd rather be a doormat or walk away than engage in an argument.

_____ Can't say I've ever been in conflict with anyone, because I rarely stay in relationships long enough to disagree.

_____ I actually enjoy conflict. Maybe too much. In a dysfunctional way, chaos and drama fuel me.

_____ I'm learning when to press and when to let something go. I seem to be getting better at engaging conflict without ending the relationship.

TIME

_____ I'm a "go-getter" kind of person. I like my list to be long and schedule to be full.

_____ I'm a self-proclaimed procrastinator. I mean well, I really do.

_____ I make plans but can rarely keep them. I disappoint people often because I break my commitments.

_____ My high-intensity workload and ability to take on a lot at once is beginning to put a strain on important relationships in my life.

SPIRITUAL

_____ I've learned to make time with God a daily priority. How much time differs on the day, but not a day goes by that I don't spend some time in prayer or Bible reading.

_____ I have good intentions when it comes to deepening my relationship with God. But church consistency and Bible reading overwhelms me until I end up doing nothing.

_____ I've put in the work of understanding how God has specifically wired me to serve him and others. I feel confident in my spiritual gifting and have others in my life who affirm that gifting.

Day *2*
Right Delights

Read the following passages of noted women of faith. Use the space below each passage to list a few key words that would likely describe their personality if you were to meet them today.

Deborah

Look up and read Judges 4:4–5, 14; 5:1, 31.

Martha

Look up and read Luke 10:38–42.

Woman at the well

Look up and read John 4:15–18, 27–30.

While we can't predict the future, we can read the patterns of the past to see how God has marked us for his purposes. Those patterns become most clear to us through the lens of our personality: the unshakeable desires of our heart that overflow in to the way we spend our time, our tone of voice, how we engage or avoid conflict, and how we overcompensate or withdraw in times of misunderstanding.

As we learn to read the patterns of our personality, we gain an understanding of God's will and calling for our life.

If your personality reveals the desires of your heart, what does your personality say you desire most?

1. Based on the pattern of my investment (or lack thereof) in intimate friendships, I desire: _____.

2. Based on the pattern of my emotional awareness and expressing/withholding my feelings, I desire: _____.

3. Based on the way I most often spend my time, I desire: _____

_____.

4. Based on my approach to engaging/avoiding difficult conversations, I desire:

_____.

5. Based on how often I spend time in God's Word, I desire: _____

_____.

> "Trust in the LORD and do good;
> dwell in the land and enjoy safe pasture.
> Take delight in the LORD,
> and he will give you the desires of your heart.
> Commit your way to the LORD;
> trust in him and he will do this."
>
> **Psalm 37:3–5**

When God gives us the desires of our heart, he will not contradict his own personality and nature. In other words, there are a lot of desires in our hearts that are impure and unwise because they do not align with the character of God.

Only by enjoying God will our heart align with the predetermined will of God. His plan for this universe has never stopped rolling down the tracks, no matter how much humans whine or refuse it. A liberating peace washes over us when we realize how little God needs us in order to accomplish his purposes.

Romans 12:2 tells us specifically how to access the desires of God and bring them into alignment with ours. Please write the verse below:

_____

_____

_____

What is one "pattern" of your past that has conformed/easily conforms to the secular world? Please describe why you know this to be true:

_____

_____

List three ways you could "renew your mind" this week if you really wanted to:

1. _____

2. _____

3. _____

As you consider "mind renewal" even at this very moment, what selfish/ungodly desire is tempting you to just stay the way you are? What scares you most about changing and/or being wrong about yourself?

_____

_____

_____

_____

As a Christian, we are not working to get into God's favor. We are already in his favor, rock-solid through our faith in Christ. But now, we've got some renewing to do.

Colossians 3:10 tells us, "[You] have put on the new self, which is being renewed in knowledge after the image of its creator."

If you are a Christian, you have already put on the new person. So, when you read Romans 12:2, view it in the context of your identity in Christ that is sealed and fixed regardless of your personality or patterns. Realize that your mind is different than your thoughts and you can have a thought without it changing your mind. This is why many people are saved and going to heaven when they die yet continue to struggle in habitual patterns of sin on earth.

When we "renew our minds," we actually feel and respond differently to our thoughts. In a truly renewed mind, "testing and approving God's will" is not merely thinking about the "right" things but loving the will of God so much that we spontaneously and naturally align with the "right" things even when we are not thinking about them.

Without a healthy understanding of how our desires are being communicated through our personality, we will never know if we are functioning out of a repetitious pattern of thought, or from a deeply transformed and renewed mind.

What is one pattern of thought you learned growing up that continues to replay itself in your life even now? Describe a pattern that feels "right" but may not be _renewed_.

_____

_____

_____

_____

Day
Feeling Our Way

Begin today's study by reading Psalm 139.

Answer the following questions based on what you read.

1. According to David, does God know our past, present, or future? _____

2. Where can we go to escape God's presence? _____

3. According to this psalm, are humans random space particles who have evolved over time or intricate designs who were formed before time? _____

4. Does David know that he is loved a little bit, most of the time, or very well?

_____

5. Is the day of our death contingent upon us, undecided, or predetermined?

_____

6. Although beautiful, what about this passage makes clear that David still has painful, hard things going on in his life?

_____

7. In light of his problems, what specifically does David ask God to do at the end of the psalm?

_____

What feelings or thoughts surface as you think of the magnitude of this psalm—as you consider the absolute control and sovereignty God has over your life? Does it scare you in an "awe-inspiring/risk everything on the chance that he's real" kind of way, or in a "panic-inducing/trusting him means I risk everything" kind of way?

_____

_____

_____

_____

The beauty of this psalm is how integrated and whole it is—capturing the big, eternal context of God as one who sees everything and is everywhere, but also as the intimate, affectionate Father who sees behind the curtain of desires into the details of our lives.

God is not trying to trick us. He has no intention for us to dismiss, deny, or water down any part of our experience. But instead, he wants us to study our past; pay attention to all parts of us, not just the ones that make us feel comfortable.

Fill in the blanks to the following verse.

Acts 17:25–28 NIV

" 25And he is not served by human hands, as if he needed anything. Rather, he himself
_____ everyone life and breath and everything else. 26From one
man he _____ all the nations, that they should inhabit the whole
earth; and he _____ their appointed times in history and the
boundaries of their lands. 27God did this so that they would _____
him and perhaps reach out for him and _____ him, though he is not far
from any one of us. 28'For in him we live and move and have our being.'"

Verse 27 translates differently depending on your version of the Bible. "Seek" or
"feel" him are common. Both words translate the same in context. But I'd like to take
a moment to focus in on the word "feel."

Feel = {from the Greek word psélaphaó}
pronounced (psay-laf-ah'-o)
meaning: to handle, to touch on the surface, to discover through personal
investigation

Our feelings are another way to identify who we are, based on what we value.

Emotions point us to the heart of our truth and treasure.

Feelings help us get a reading on our belief at any given moment but cannot be allowed
to guide our beliefs. Why? Because they change rapidly in level of intensity depending
on: the time of day, how much sleep or caffeine we've had, and with whom we are in
the room.

Feelings flow and talk to us all the time, 24/7—even through our subconscious dream
states. Our feelings may be accurate or just be a spontaneous reaction that mirrors
the way our grandmother felt about the same thing.

Write a few words below about how you were taught to handle emotions/feelings as a child, teenager, and young adult.

_____

_____

What is one, specific thing God may be trying to say to you through the following life-spots:

- Who you are married to (if married):

_____

_____

- The personal "issues" confided to you by your (coworker, roommate, best friend):

_____

_____

- The neighborhood (area) where you live:

_____

_____

● If you have children, the personality/personalities of your child/children:

_____

_____

_____

● The home-life you grew up in:

_____

_____

_____

God is using our emotional states to tell us the truth about our eternal state.

God wants us to stop worrying so much about why and what other people are doing, and instead to think deeply about why and what we are doing.

The more self-aware we are, the more interconnected and unified we will be to the Holy Spirit—giving the "others" in our sphere of influence a reason to trust us. The goal of our interconnectedness in feeling and spirit is, yes, oneness within ourselves, a whole sense of being and presence, but also, and just as important to God, our ability to give that wholeness away to others in relationship. And because we can't give away what we don't own for ourselves, it is impossible to expect other people to respond in rational, healthy ways, if we are not also responding in rational, healthy ways.

Day 4
Taking Inventory

Using the seven emotional categories on pages 138–139, complete the following inventory.

I strongly encourage you to write something in each box (key words, example story, etc.) despite how uncomfortable or silly this exercise may seem.

EMOTIONAL INVENTORY KEY

CAUSE:

The person, place, word, or experience that most often evokes/triggers this feeling in your life.

EFFECT:

Your emotional, behavioral response to this cause. This could be what you do (i.e., shut down, isolate, defend), who or what you turn to (i.e., television, friend), or where your thoughts go (i.e., I remember when my dad . . .). Just write the true effect as you most often experience it. This is not about whether the effect is "bad" or "good."

SELF-NEED:

The thing you are seeking most in the moment of that particular emotional state (i.e., satisfaction, peace, pity, acknowledgment, comfort, justice, etc.).

GOD-SPEAK:

What could God be trying to say to you through this specific emotion? (i.e., "you have unresolved pain here," "you are doubting me," "there is need for reconciliation with her," "I thought you could use a good laugh," etc.).

ANGER: hostility, fury, annoyance, frustration, injustice, misunderstood	
CAUSE	
EFFECT	
SELF-NEED	
GOD-SPEAK	

ANXIETY: apprehension, nervousness, scared	
CAUSE	
EFFECT	
SELF-NEED	
GOD-SPEAK	

SHAME: guilt, regret, embarrassment, humiliation	
CAUSE	
EFFECT	
SELF-NEED	
GOD-SPEAK	

HAPPINESS: thrill, delight, joy, peace, contentment	
CAUSE	
EFFECT	
SELF-NEED	
GOD-SPEAK	

AFFECTION: belonging, acceptance, intimacy, ecstasy	
CAUSE	
EFFECT	
SELF-NEED	
GOD-SPEAK	

DISGUST: contempt, aversion, dislike, offensive	
CAUSE	
EFFECT	
SELF-NEED	
GOD-SPEAK	
SADNESS: grief, loneliness, despair, self-pity	
CAUSE	
EFFECT	
SELF-NEED	
GOD-SPEAK	

In **Matthew 15:18–19,** Jesus tells us exactly what comes out of our heart:

"But the things that come out of a person's _____ come from the heart, and these defile them. For out of the heart come _____ —murder, adultery, sexual immorality, theft, false testimony, slander.

● Read **Ephesians 4:17–19**, then explain what a mind disconnected from God is like:

● Now read **Ephesians 4:25–32**. Describe a heart interconnected to the Spirit of God:

● According to **Ephesians 4:20–24**, there are three access points to move from a divided heart to a whole heart.

1. Assuming we know Jesus, remember what he has taught us and don't act the same way we did before we knew him (vs. 20–22).

2. Let God change our minds and attitudes (vs. 23).

3. Be sure that what we take in (put on) and give to others (wear) reflects our true self—an identity created in holy likeness (vs. 24).

In Christ, we are not who we once were. We no longer need to settle for old, boring, unfulfilling ways of resolving conflict, engaging relationships, or encountering our emotion. But this "newness" does not mean we shut down or regulate our feelings. Instead, God invites us to think deeply about *why* we feel the way we feel—take a step back to breathe, ponder our past, and respond from our renewed emotional state.

When trigger-points hit us and old wounds resurface, God does not want us to dismiss them; He wants us to embrace them. *His new life assures us that we have strength enough to feel big feelings from our past without allowing them to dictate our future.*

Remember,

Renewal requires something old to work with.

Based on your inventory, what is one feeling toward a specific person or experience that has been renewed by God? Give a specific example of a past "trigger point," and how you now respond differently than you once did.

_____

_____

_____

_____

_____

_____

_____

Day 5
Sobering Gifts

According to 1 Corinthians 12:1, what should we be informed about?

_____

According to Romans 1:11, the purpose of our spiritual gifts is:

_____

Perhaps our struggle to trust God with our past is not so much our not knowing our spiritual gift as it is the more basic problem of not desiring to strengthen the faith of others. Human nature is prone to tear down rather than build up. Sit two toddlers in the center of a room with one toy and you will see how engrained our selfish, sinful nature is. With little direction from our parents or life experience, our own hearts default to choose ourselves first.

I believe this is why Jesus says the greatest command is to "love your neighbor as yourself" (Matthew 22:39). Because we love ourselves a lot.

We shouldn't get too caught up trying to figure out what our specific gift or calling might be, until we first decide to use it for others. You can see the rub with our modern day cheers for "self-love," "self-care," and "self-help." If we chant this first, it is likely we will miss our true purpose altogether.

The Bible teaches us to receive and claim specific abilities and giftings over our lives. But we must not miss the aim of our gifting—to encourage the faith of someone else. Look up and read Romans 12:3–8.

What is the word used to measure the distribution of our gifts (vs. 6)? _____

The Bible teaches that both the gifts we have and the faith to use them are _given_ to us by God in varying measure. This sobering truth is meant to do just that—sober any lofty notion within us that we are "great," "talented," or "gifted" because of anything we have done. Paul gives us this warning that we would learn not to boast in our accomplishments or become self-reliant, but instead humbly desire more of God's doling out of our giftedness by surrendering our desires to him in increasing measure each day.

What is one thing you are really good at? I'm serious. Don't be self-deprecating. Are you good at time management, parenting, cooking, studying, running a business? What is one skill/talent that has always been with you as something you enjoy and are often asked to do?

_____

Has this talent ever gotten the best of you? In other words, can you describe a time in your life when you forgot it was given to you by God, and instead used it to rely on yourself? If so, describe how God "knocked the props" out from under this way of existing with your gift?

_____

_____

_____

Read 1 Peter 4:10–11 and answer TRUE or FALSE to the following statements:

1. Spiritual gifting is only for a FEW people. **TRUE / FALSE**

2. We can serve others well, even when the amount of GRACE to trust God varies from person to person. **TRUE / FALSE**

3. When we serve in our gifting, although given by God, we are still limited by our mortality. **TRUE / FALSE**

To the degree we have received **grace** for ourselves is the degree we will **see** God enough to **serve** others.

*If grace is God's unconditional love for us, how do **you** display your unconditional love for others in the area of your calling/service?*

_____

_____

_____

_____

There is nothing more thrilling, more joyful, more meaningful, more satisfying than to find our niche in the eternal unfolding of God's glory. Our gift may seem small, but as a part of the revelation of God's infinite glory, it takes on a whole new life and meaning.

3 ACCESS POINTS TO YOUR CALLING

The Bible does not explicitly tell us how to be sure, once and for all, that we are gifted and/or called to a certain task or responsibility. Freedom is more fluid than that. Our giftedness can change depending on the need of the season. Our personalities should change based on our spiritual maturity. And our callings shift that God may continue to increase our faith in him.

However, the overall context of the Bible points to three specific access points to our calling that we are wise to investigate and practically nurture.

#1 DESIRE

> "Whatever you do, work at it with all your heart, as working for the Lord, not for human masters."
>
> **Colossians 3:23**

At the end of the day, there is one thing (or multiple things) we would do if money were no object and we had zero fear of rejection. What is your passion, your desire? What do you absolutely love to do and know beyond a shadow of a doubt, you were born to do it? (i.e., be a mother, teach, nurture others to health, care for animals, etc.)

_____

_____

#2 ABILITY

> "He has filled them with skill to do all kinds of work as engravers, designers, embroiderers in blue, purple and scarlet yarn and fine linen, and weavers—all of them skilled workers and designers."
>
> **Exodus 35:35**

One of our greatest motivations to know ourselves is to be sure of our ability. We are not designed to do all things good, but instead designed to do a few things well. What is your natural ability? Please describe the areas of your work/service that come easy to you.

_____

_____

#3 OPPORTUNITY

> "Then he continued, 'Do not be afraid, Daniel. Since the first day that you set your mind to gain understanding and to humble yourself before your God, your words were heard, and I have come in response to them. But the prince of the Persian

kingdom resisted me **twenty-one** days. Then Michael, one of
the chief princes, came to help me, because I was detained
there with the king of Persia. Now I have come to explain
to you what will happen to your people in the future.'"

Daniel 10:12–14

In a practical sense, there are times in our lives when we feel ready, prepared, and able to perform a certain task or serve in a particular area, and yet, the opportunity simply does not present itself. What is one area of your sphere of influence where you feel ready to serve, but practically speaking, there is no available opportunity?

Listen to God's voice in your life. It will give you countless words that describe your way of being, relating, and engaging others. These words will help you identify your character and your role in life. Listen to your stories. They reveal a pattern of roles that you've played throughout your life and are meant to play now.

Our callings are not a "to-do list" we need to check off. Our gifts are not the end goal, but a process of working out the nature of God within us.

God is using every part of you—your oddities, inflections of speech, the street you grew up on, your first job, and how you style your hair—to speak to you. To make known something about himself that will only be known through *your* unique face, personality, and story.

Don't be afraid to listen to your life.

WEEK 6

GOD DOESN'T WASTE YOUR CONFESSION

This is a great week to read chapters 17–18 in the book!

Introduction (7 MINUTES)

Leader, please read aloud to group:

Each week has been leading us to this very moment. Not as an end or finale, but as a beginning, a *hope* that has called to me on my darkest days. The days I wanted to quit, lay it down, stop fighting for truth and instead, let my mind sink lethargically into social media submission.

Sisters, if we want to be healed, if we want to experience real freedom in this life, then there's just got to come a time when we shout, "Enough already!" You and I, together, must *fight* to close the gap between what we think we know and what is real. The gap between "play-pretend" Christian and a woman who lives her life in joyful submission to Christ. The gap between believing *in* God and actually *believing* him.

Confession closes the gap and makes us confident in our own skin.

Our confession tells us the "true story," bringing dark things to light in a way that heals us from the inside-out and liberates us from all our unanswered questions. In the most honest place of our heart, we can finally lay claim to the grace that's been ours all along!

Confession is the only way I will walk away from a decade of work piled up in this offering, lay it on the altar of surrender, let God burn up the bits where I've missed it, or could have said it better, and gladly walk away to keep on living my life! Oh yes, I will think about you, reader. I will wonder if you still like me at the end of this; love me even, as I do you.

But the confessions I've made remind me I'll also be okay if you don't. The dark things I've placed in the light no longer have power over me. Purpose, yes. But not power.

I will choose to continue to be a woman who believes no part of her life is an accident or disappointment. But instead, a life story from a God who authored every scene on purpose, for purpose.

I'd make you so uncomfortable with a full-frontal hug right now if I could. Because I can't do any of this alone. I *need* you to believe this *with* me! To keep on asking yourself hard questions, sharing your story, seeking out good people to love you, and above all, holding tight to your Bible as though your life depended on it. Because it does.

Don't let this study be the end. Let it be your beginning. Look for him in all your unlikely places, *and* in the unlikely places of others. Help others see him in the dark!

Because he sees you. He loves you, wants you, and is going to chase after you until you finally take him up on who he's always been.

I love you. I really do.

Video Session Six (24 MINUTES)

Watch Video Session 6 and fill in the blanks below.

1. Problem: Humans insist on bringing God into _____ instead of receiving his as our own.

2. God has no desire to redefine our lives _____ from people and experiences.

3. God walks through the back door of our lives and requests one thing: _____

_____

> **Here I am! I stand at the door and knock. If anyone hears my voice and opens the door, I will come in and eat with that person, and they with me.**
>
> **Revelation 3:20**

4. Bondage will always reveal itself in the _____ of our lives—behaviorally and emotionally.

5. When we fear _____, we will not experience the _____ love of God.

6. The moment we feel too sad to receive God's grace is the moment we know we've stayed too long in the _____.

7. God is not merely tolerating us. He wholeheartedly _____.

HE'S ON OUR SIDE.

Use this space to take notes of your own:

_____

_____

_____

_____

_____

_____

_____

_____

_____

Group Discussion Questions (30 MINUTES)

1. What big themes or patterns of your life have revealed God to you? Please describe one specific characteristic of God that has become more real to you through a certain life-marking experience.

2. What is one way you would like to serve those who have suffered the same way you have suffered in life?

3. If you have not done so already, what specific fear do you still need to address in order to give yourself permission to share your story with another?

4. Confession brings to light not only the harmful things we have done to others but any lingering resentment or bitterness we have for those who've harmed us. Is there a person you are scared to confront because it will be difficult to forgive them?

5. What's one thing that excites you about bringing *all* of your junk to the surface? Share how you think it would feel to fully live the most honest version of yourself.

SESSION 6 FOCUS

God does not waste our confession.

He uses the most honest version of us to set us free.

In the light of day, our deepest struggles may still be weaknesses, but they can no longer be used against us.

Closing Prayer

(lead out or ask a volunteer)

Points of prayer for Session Six:

- To trust God is faithful and just to purify us from ALL our sins, not just a few (1 John 1:9).

- Strength to reject the pride in us that seeks blame, isolation, or desire to be right.

- Patience to let God search *all* our heart for lurking darkness, even the things we think we've already dealt with.

- Wisdom to judge correctly between the things we've already confessed and that which we haven't.

- Clarity and commitment to next steps of reconciliation or restitution God will most likely ask of us through our confession.

PERSONAL BIBLE STUDY Session 6

GOD DOESN'T WASTE YOUR CONFESSION

Day 1
Unnecessary Punishment

> "There is no fear in love, but perfect love casts out fear. For fear has to do with punishment, and whoever fears has not been perfected in love."
>
> **1 John 4:18**

Think back to any time your love has been rejected or dismissed simply because you could not live up to an expectation. Think about that person who always seems to *need* something from you—an acknowledgment, an invite, an apology, attention, your life on their terms.

Do these relationships feel light and free? Or heavy and hindered? Do you find yourself drawing near to "needy" people or doing your best to avoid them without hurting their feelings?

The "conditions" we build around our love lurk in both the intentional and unintentional wrinkles of life: a passive-aggressive comment, a shift in tone or posture, a sudden or slow withdrawal from spending time with a person, faking it, withholding affection to maintain control, or manipulating affection to get what we want.

Conditional love—it sucks the life from us and others.

Unconditional love, however, releases us and others from expectation or need.

Unconditional, perfect love is rare and hard to come by because of the enormous amount of self-awareness and self-denial it requires. To love others as God loves us demands daily, sometimes hourly, self-reflection of our motives.

Perfect love is all we want in life, yet it's the most unnatural thing about our life. To receive it, we must never stop asking ourselves to do hard things. To give it, we must stop asking others to do hard things.

Briefly describe a relationship when you offered your love to another, secretly hoping they would meet a certain need in your life. Describe the expectation you later realized you had for them, although unintentional.

_____

_____

_____

Briefly describe a time when you offered your unconditional love to another without any expectation or need, only to have it denied or used against you.

_____

_____

_____

Love contingencies we've written for our lives can be unintentional, but they should not be unapproachable.

We have to be willing to stare our greatest fears right in their ugly face. We must drill down to the bottom of the way we give and receive love based on conditions we've created to protect us from being hurt.

Anywhere we expect or need a return on our love is a stronghold of fear in our lives, creating unnecessary punishment for ourselves and others.

So, let's do some drilling. Time for a bit of honest self-evaluation.

Place a check mark next to any statement on page 156 that accurately describes a feeling or behavior you have consistently experienced over the past thirty days. If any of these statements ring true, you are most likely subjecting yourself to the unnecessary punishment of fear.

Reminder, this part is about you and no one else, which makes it more painful. Don't let pride dictate your honesty.

_____ I feel anxious when I see text-reply dots on my phone. If the dots take too long or disappear after being there for several seconds, I feel a twinge of panic that I have done or said something wrong until they reply.

_____ When a friend cancels or no-shows a plan we committed to together, I get angry. I stop talking to her or withdraw until she acknowledges my disappointment.

_____ I only truly enjoy a getaway, vacation, or night out if I plan it.

_____ If a friend fails to return my email, text, or phone call in the amount of time I think they should, I begin listing reasons in my head why I don't really want to be their friend in the first place.

_____ When I am approached by someone telling me how I have hurt them, or how I could be wrong about them, I immediately take a posture of defense.

_____ Even though it's been years, I think about this person every single day. I am furious and hurt that they have never apologized or acknowledged my feelings.

_____ I avoid certain areas or establishments in my town because I do not want to chance running into him/her.

Jesus did not die for us to live in fear of painful experiences or people. We need not guard our own love with contingencies and conditions. Instead, we are to receive God's love in joy and awe (good fear), not in anger or self-loathing (bad fear).

On the cross, Jesus carried the weight of the punishment we deserve. With his death, he cast out fear, and with his life, draws us near.

> **"For God's will was for us to be made holy by the sacrifice of the body of Jesus Christ, once for all time."**
> **Hebrews 10:10 NLT**

As a Christian, the gap between us and God has been closed with the outstretched arms of Jesus.

In him, we never, not once, receive punishment for our sin. We will, however, experience the natural repercussions of any behavior tempting us or others to turn away from the unconditional love of God.

Receiving consequence for our careless words and behaviors is to be expected. Not only expected but welcomed as a discipline of God's grace—drawing us back to a love that trusts him and leads others to trust him.

According to Proverbs 3:11–12, who does God discipline? _____

According to Hebrews 12:8–10, why does God discipline?

_____

Knowing the difference between discipline and punishment is a big step in our spiritual maturity.

You can remember it like this:

Discipline draws in, punishment casts out.

This week, I encourage you to be as self-aware as possible when it comes to what or who triggers anxiety, worry, or fear. Ask yourself, *"When I feel this way, do I want to* **draw near to God** *for accountability, or,* **run from God** *to avoid punishment?"*

Because of Jesus, God draws you to himself. The closer you get to his love, the more frequently you release yourself and others from the unnecessary expectation of conditional love.

Day 2
Approaching God

Can you identify specific ways you relate to others that also reflects the way you relate to God? This can be a particular behavior, attitude, approach, level of vulnerability, or way you engage conflict.

_____

_____

_____

Read Hebrews 4:16 to learn how God wants us to relate to him.

● In this verse, what specifically are we approaching? _____

● With what attitude do we approach? _____

● Why are we approaching him? _____

● When should we approach him? _____

Confidence = {from the Greek word *parre'sia*}

  meaning—*freedom, openness—especially in speech, boldness, resolve, to be taken seriously*

Do you *confidently* relate to God? Perhaps I should back up and ask, do you approach God at all?

When we finally cry out to God, we do so from a place of deficiency. We lack the one thing only *he* can give—*love without condition.*

We **confidently** approach God, because we are **confident** he loves us without needing anything from us.

God doesn't need our prayers, our good behavior, our church attendance, or even our love. He has no need, lack, or deficiency as humans do. God is complete and perfect in and of himself—the *source* of love. God is not reactive to our behaviors; he is not waiting for us to "do" the right thing in order to bless us. God is not surprised or disappointed when we distrust him.

Look up and Read 1 John 4:15–18.

Consider why God's love is **perfect and without punishment**.

Take this to heart . . .

- Confessing (acknowledging or remembering) the sacrifice of Jesus Christ on the cross positions our hearts and minds to receive the unconditional love of God (vs. 15).

- As we receive God's love, our soul is at rest. In this state of abiding, fear is incapacitated (vs. 16).

- Where fear is incapacitated, confidence is replicated. The more confident we are in our relationship with God, the more often we will receive and give perfect love (vs. 17).

God will never use our honesty against us.

Briefly describe your natural, instinctive reaction when the particular fear noted below is triggered. For example, *"When I fear rejection, I push people away before they get the chance to reject me."* Or, *"When I fear change, I dig my heels in deeper where I am and rarely ask for help."*

Note: There is no need to air dirty laundry unless it's stinking up the joint. The goal here is to be honest with yourself and identify the lies holding you back from confidently approaching God. Your reaction to any one of these "fears" could last only seconds or linger for months.

A natural gut reaction can also look like, *"When it comes to the unknown, I thank God he already knows and that's enough for me! I choose to trust him and move on with my day."*

PRESENTING FEAR	MY GUT REACTION
REJECTION	
INTIMACY	
LOSS OF CONTROL	
FAILURE	
NEED FOR CHANGE	
UNKNOWN	
OPINIONS OF OTHERS	

As far as our minds are concerned, the memories that fire together wire together. Most of our reactive fear is hard-wired into us based on the way those closest to us handled their fears.

What we *think* we know is tremendously important to God. Fill in the blanks below to acknowledge God's design and desire for our **MINDS**.

Proverbs 19:21 ESV

" _____ are the plans in the mind of a man, but it is the purpose of the LORD that will _____ ."

Isaiah 26:3 ESV

"You keep him in perfect _____ whose mind is stayed on you, because he trusts in you."

Matthew 22:37 ESV

"Love the Lord your God with all your _____ and with all your _____ and with all your _____."

Romans 8:6

"The mind governed by the flesh is _____, but the mind governed by the Spirit is _____ and _____."

Romans 12:2

"Do not conform to the pattern of this world, but be transformed by the _____ of your mind."

Hebrews 8:10

"This is the covenant I will establish with the people of Israel after that time, declares the Lord: I will put my laws in their minds and _____ them on their hearts."

Knowing *what* you fear is healthy. Knowing *why* you fear is deliverance.

Identifying how we approach God, realizing how we relate to others, helps us peel back the layers of our *what* to get to the bigger question of *why*.

Day 3
Collective Confession

All of us experience the fear of man to some degree.

Read Proverbs 29:25. Why does this verse tell us the fear of man is so lethal?

The Hebrew word for "snare" in this passage is the same as "trap"—as in, used for hunting and catching. Think about that word picture for a moment. A good trap, one intended to catch something, is designed with much skill and intention; often camouflaged—hiding in plain sight. A trap lures—it uses something desirable to draw in its victim. Finally, a trap closes shut—it gives just enough freedom for its prey to flail, claw, and fight, without being released. Often, the victim is only left to exhaust itself into a lifeless, paralyzed state.

Does any of this strike a heart-string with you? Or perhaps, if you're like me, throw a throat chop? As always, the Lord is quick to show us the way to escape.

Based on Proverbs 29:25, what is the opposite of fearing man?

List one *relationship* in your life that would change right now if you really believed you were safe with God, despite the opinion of men and women?

One *decision* that would change . . .

One *feeling* that would change . . .

_____

Have you ever loved a lie so much that you prefer to believe it? Do you punish or sabotage yourself because the snare has become more comfortable than freedom? Briefly describe this time in your life.

_____

_____

_____

_____

Safe = {someone who will not use our honesty against us}

The desire to "feel safe" is common language these days, but what are we really asking for in terms of relationship?

Acceptance, vulnerability, trust, no expectations, no games. This is what we want from people—to feel safe with our love and honesty. To confess our worst-case scenario without being rejected, and to say out loud the worst thing we've ever done without it being used against us.

According to James 5:16, is the confession of our sins just between us and God, or are others involved in this process?

_____

According to this verse, what is the goal of confession? _____

But are we to trust just "anyone" with our most sacred places? What type of person is to join us for confession? _____

List at least three people in your life who you would consider "safe" by this definition. People you could open up with and talk to about your deepest struggles or darkest secrets:

_____

If you are unable to think of at least three trustworthy, righteous people in your life right now, why do you think this is?

_____

_____

When we open up our story to another person, despite our leeriness or fear, we are not choosing the easiest road, but we are choosing the best one.

Confession to another Christian also guards us from justifying ourselves out of true repentance (see 2 Corinthians 7:10).

Interesting that God uses the one thing that can so quickly lead to fear to set us free from fear—relationship. Yes, of course God hears and accepts your confession before you utter one word of it aloud, and yet he commands us to engage our honesty in a real, relational way with the flesh and blood of other people. Why? Because he is in the business of redeeming all things, our past, our pain, and the feelings around the thing we fear most—honest relationships.

Confession is not about broadcasting our sins or airing our dirty laundry on a microphone or platform. But it does mean, believers need to be known openly and deeply as members of one another, one body (see Ephesians 4:25).

> "Fight the good fight of the faith. Take hold of the
> eternal life to which you were called when you made your
> *good confession* in the presence of many witnesses."
> **1 Timothy 6:12, emphasis mine**

Day 4
Toward the Light

> "Search me, God, and know my heart;
> test me and know my anxious thoughts.
> See if there is any offensive way in me,
> and lead me in the way everlasting."
>
> **Psalm 139:23–24**

What two things is David asking God to KNOW about him?

1. _____

2. _____

What is the "direction" of David's heart that he is asking God to call out?

_____

This conversation between God and David is one of the Bible's greatest examples of how we are to approach and follow through with confession in a way that works! A way that sets us free to now use all the parts of our uprooted past for the future glory of God.

Step 1 of Confession: **Access Personal Fear**

I would be willing to bet that 90 percent of our anxiety and worry comes from borrowed drama—chaos we bring on ourselves by studying the lives of others, when we should be critiquing our own.

Most of the fear that cripples us could be alleviated simply by taking our focus off what others are doing. David is right to approach the Lord with, "search *me*—test *me*." Instead of "fix him—change her."

When fear attacks, play the defense by searching yourself. While in defense mode, here is a list of helpful questions to ask yourself:

- Why am I anxious?

- Do I have any selfish or sinful desire inside me that is fully, partly, or even 1 percent to blame for this?

- Do I owe someone an apology?

- Am I scared of a person, place, or thing?

Here is a list of people/things you should *not* consult to help answer the above questions:

- Social media.

- The economy.

- Political leaders.

- Pop culture.

- Your kids.

- A friend who is going through a particularly painful/hard season of their own.

God acknowledges that you will experience fear when it comes to surfacing painful parts of your past. He already knows the loss, devastating betrayal, and agonizing sadness that you will feel due to life-altering seasons of grief. Remember, God is not asking you *not* to fear; he is simply asking you to fear the right thing—him.

Fill in the blanks of the following verses:

"Work out your _____ with fear and trembling, for it is God who works in you." Philippians 2:12–13

"And thus, let us offer to God acceptable worship, with _____
_____, for our God is a consuming fire." Hebrews 12:28–29 ESV

"The Spirit of the LORD shall rest upon him. The Spirit of wisdom and understanding, the Spirit of counsel and might, the Spirit of knowledge and the fear of the LORD. And his _____ shall be in the _____ of the LORD." Isaiah 11:2–3 ESV

Step 2 of Confession: Begin with Yourself

"Therefore, if you are offering your gift at the altar and there remember that your brother or sister has something against you, leave your gift there in front of the altar. First go and be reconciled to them; then come and offer your gift" (Matthew 5:23–24).

According to Matthew 5:23–24, what actions are we to take the moment we are aware someone has been offended or hurt by us.

_____ Pray about it.

_____ Go to church.

_____ Talk it through with friends first.

_____ Talk ourselves out of it.

_____ Drop everything and go to that person.

Here is an example of how to approach an offense after searching your own heart:

"I don't like the direction our relationship is going. Here is how I can see I have personally contributed to the problem. Where else do you feel I have wronged you?"

Then, listen well to the criticism you've invited.

Always assume God is speaking to you through this painful situation and is showing you ways to be more careful or change. Assume that God is speaking to you even through your flaws and theirs.

Is there a current relationship that needs this approach from you? Explain how you will commit to approach this person differently and why this relationship is worth restoring.

_____

_____

_____

_____

If there is even an inkling of possibility that we have hurt someone, we must go to them. And when we go, we must be ready to admit our wrong without excuses and without blaming the circumstances.

Step 3 of Confession: Forgive

Forgiveness = {refusing to seek payment for the wrong done to us, and instead absorbing the debt to ourselves}

The reason why so much of our honesty with one another stops short is because we forget how costly it is to forgive. To forgive someone places us in voluntary suffering.

Here are a few indicators that true forgiveness has not been extended to another, and that it's time for us to volunteer some time:

- We continue to bring up the way they hurt us.

- We talk to others about the way they hurt us.

- We are more demanding and controlling with them than we are with others.

- We avoid them and have grown cold toward them.

"Then the master called the servant in. 'You wicked servant,' he said, 'I canceled all that debt of yours because you begged me to. Shouldn't you have had mercy on your fellow servant

*just as I had on you?' In anger his master handed him over to the jailers to be tortured, until he should pay back all he owed. "This is how my heavenly Father will treat each of you unless you forgive your brother or sister **from your heart**." Matthew 18:32–35, emphasis mine*

Real forgiveness, from-the-heart-forgiveness, is not a feeling. It is a choice. In light of Jesus' torment on our behalf, there is no offense we are not equipped to forgive.

Don't forget—forgiveness is not contingent on reconciliation. Sometimes, due to death or a move, a danger to life or unresponsiveness from the other party, restoring the relationship is not possible. But that does not mean true forgiveness is impossible. In most cases of painful wounding, we are called to forgive, pursue reconciliation as far as we can practically take it, and then wait out the rest through prayer and obedience as we continue to trust him more.

Who do you need to forgive, truly? Is there someone still on the hook of apology or owing? Even if they are unwilling to take ownership of their wrong, describe your next step to releasing them from your thoughts. What kind of voluntary suffering will this look like on your part?

_____

_____

_____

_____

Day 5
Take It!

Read Luke 7:36–50 to complete this statement:

The identifying mark of a person who knows how to give and receive real LOVE is the person who also knows real _____.

According to the Bible, there are three types of people in the world: those who believe they are too "good" for forgiveness, those who believe they are too "bad" for forgiveness, and those who know they need forgiveness and have joyfully received it. The final category of people, I believe, are the happiest in the world.

Those of us instinctively aware that we are both in need and full at the same time are of the most passionate and compassionate on the planet!

Which category of people does your life reflect you most often align yourself with?

Too Good   **Too Bad**   **Need It–Got It**

How we "cover" ourselves up looks differently from person to person, but the truth is, all of us, deep down, know we want to hide, to cover up how we've failed or may fail another if we get too close. It doesn't matter the culture or century, we are all acutely aware there is something wrong with us, a need or deficiency within.

Wouldn't it be fabulous to finally admit that? To once and for all be at peace with the fact that, to some extent, we will never get it all together this side of heaven?

Look up and read Psalm 32:1–2.

According to this passage, what is the state/condition of those whose sins are forgiven, covered, and not counted against them?

To really breathe in this truth as our reality, we cannot ignore the original Hebrew and Greek meaning of "blessed" in the Bible. Our English language waters down the word "blessed" to a simple state of being inspired, encouraged, gifted, or favored. But the Bible renders "blessing" as something far more glorious to behold. To be "blessed" in the Bible literally means to be *whole*, complete wellness of being and profound fulfillment.

Describe what it would look like, practically, for you to experience BLESSING as God intends. What about your life needs to change for "complete wellness of being" to become your reality?

_____

_____

_____

Notice in the psalm WHO in particular receives this _whole_ kind of blessing?

THE ONE WHO IS _____

There is a difference between true and false guilt before God. False guilt is self-pity. And self-pity keeps people on a loop of confession with no real change in their lives.

Now Read Psalm 32:5.

Notice how many times you see the word "my" or "I" in this verse.

The redundancy of this verse is important! It is David's progression from self-pity to grief. Grief over the ownership of his ability to sin. He is sorry for the pain of his sin; the consequences others have endured because of his sin. He is not feeling sorry for himself for the many years of being on the receiving end of someone else's sin, which he was! Instead . . .

Next, read Psalm 32:8–9.

It's here that David receives personal counseling from the Lord. God no longer wants David to relate to him as a horse relates to a bridle, controlled by threat and the repetition of doing the same thing over and over again only because he is scared of consequences.

Finally, read Psalm 32:10–11.

Do you obey God's Word because you think you have to or because you sincerely want to? A clear indicator that you have fully laid claim to God's grace for yourself is an "upright heart" who trusts God simply because she delights to do so. What is your heart of obedience saying about you right now?

_____

_____

_____

Have you received God's grace for yourself? If yes, what specific motivation to trust him proves this to you?

_____

_____

_____

If you're not sure, what specific behavior or attitude about life causes you to question this?

_____

_____

_____

We cannot hide *in* God when we are too busy hiding *from* God.

This is why Jesus died in crucifixion. His clothes stripped from his body in a public, not private death, his arms outstretched and nailed, not allowing him to shield onlookers from his tender place of torment. Jesus was utterly exposed and dehumanized for us; stripped that we might be clothed.

Second Corinthians 5:21 tells us, "*God made him who had no sin to be sin for us, so that in him we might become the righteousness of God.*"

This is the ultimate essence of the unwasted life.

Receive for yourself what is finished, done, and complete in Christ.

If you have never made the ultimate confession, Jesus is reminding you, "Whoever acknowledges me before others, I will also acknowledge before my Father in heaven" (Matthew 10:32).

To confess our need of a Savior out loud is not weakness; it is liberation.

Here at the beginning of our end together, if there is any doubt in your mind that you have fully received the blessing of God's grace for your life, I implore you, confess it now.

Fight for that friendship. Go back to church. Look to forgive more than you look for offense. Trust God's patient work in difficult people and duck your head to no one over the regrets of your past. Choose to see purpose in your pain. Trust the theme of your story. Say yes when asked to share it.

No part of your life is wasted. God uses it all. Even the stuff you wouldn't.

> **"They will rebuild the ancient ruins**
> **and restore the places long devastated;**
> **they will renew the ruined cities**
> **that have been devastated for generations.**
>
> **"I delight greatly in the LORD;**
> **my soul rejoices in my God.**
> **For he has clothed me with garments of salvation**
> **and arrayed me in a robe of his righteousness."**
>
> **Isaiah 61:4, 10**

VIDEO NOTES ANSWER KEY

Session 1
Design
The Good Will Of God
Waste It
Location
Time In History
Parents
Experiences
Setup
Who We Are Meant To Be
Obey

Session 2
Personal
Community
Believe
Debt
Hiding Out
Rejected
New Heart
Love

Session 3
Reality
Did God Really Say
Not
Light / Dark
Honesty / Purity
Delights
Done With It

Session 4
Lingers
Convince Our Hearts
Today / Yesterday
Will / Work / Whine
Process / Point
Defeated
Position / Promise
Whole

Session 5
Imprints
Ignorance
Resist / Recognize
Satan's Schemes
Pain
Shape Of Self
Who He Is / Who We Are
Belief
Best
Suggest Our Mood
Time
Gauge / Guide
Story

Session 6
Our Image
Apart
Share A Meal With Him
Extremes
Punishment / Perfect
Dark
Wants Us

LEADER HELPS

- If you are the leader, always arrive to your group's meeting location early.

- Set the tone of welcome and excitement every time you see a group member's face.

- Focus on the time members of the group *are* putting in and encourage them there.

- Live the example of commitment by your actions, not words. Trust God to do the rest.

- Don't try to "fix" or "save" your group members. **Just love them**. Enjoy them. They will receive from this study exactly what God intends for them to receive.

Dealing with Problems in Group

Because we are all human, challenges within your group are bound to arise. The most important thing you can do as a leader is to constantly ask God for wisdom and then be faithful to his direction. The following are tips on how to effectively deal with a few of the common problems small-group leaders face:

- If a participant frequently misses group time, call, email, text, or write a note letting her know her presence is missed, desired, and valued.

- If participants are not completing their individual studies, show by example how much you, the leader, are receiving from making this time with the Lord a priority. Do not allow another's undone homework to distract or dismiss from the most important thing—their presence.

- If members are getting into heated debates over certain issues, remember that some debate is good—healthy and beneficial for growth. Disagreements and debates do not always need a resolution. You are free to move the conversation along to the next question without landing on a specific end, and with tension still hanging in the air.

- Do not pretend to know an answer if you don't. It is okay *not* to know. Encourage the group to seek out an answer and do your best to research on your own for the next meeting if you feel led to.

- If a member is sharing "prayer requests" that are actually pieces of gossip or slander, shut it down. A great way to shut down gossip is before it starts; address the group collectively before session one.

- If participants are "oversharing" during group discussion time, you might want to set a time limit for sharing.

- If members are dealing with life-threatening concerns, such as drug or alcohol abuse, sexual or physical abuse, or mental illness, do not try to take on those issues alone. The best way to help in such situations is to help a person seek out a trained professional.